20

Gluten Free Bread Machine Cookbook
For Beginners

Simple and Easy Mouthwatering
Step-by-Step Recipes for
Beginners

Megan Bates

Contents

Introduction

In a world where bread is a staple, those with gluten sensitivities or celiac disease often find themselves wishing for the comforting taste and texture of a warm, freshly baked loaf. The fight to find delicious gluten-free bread options can be frustrating and disheartening. But fear not! With the advent of bread machines, a new era of gluten-free baking has emerged, offering flavor, convenience, and a newfound sense of freedom in the kitchen.

Imagine waking up to the delicious aroma of a freshly baked loaf, knowing that it's not only safe for your dietary needs but also bursting with incredible flavors. The road to gluten-free baking mastery may seem perplexing at first, but trust me, it's a path worth exploring.

Growing up, I had always been a bread lover. The soft, pillowy texture and the irresistible taste of freshly baked bread were the epitome of comfort for me. However, as I grew older, I started experiencing unexplained health issues. After numerous doctor visits and tests, I was diagnosed with celiac disease—a condition that needs strict avoidance of gluten.

Suddenly, my beloved bread became a banned indulgence. I felt a sense of loss and wished for a solution that would allow me to enjoy the simple pleasure of a warm slice without compromising my health. That's when I stumbled upon the gluten-free bread machine—a culinary game-changer that would alter my view of gluten-free baking forever.

With a mix of excitement and skepticism, I started on my gluten-free bread machine journey. The initial burst of enthusiasm quickly gave way to excitement as I managed the complexities of gluten-free flours, binders, and rising agents. The quest for the perfect loaf was a perplexing puzzle, but I was determined to unlock the secrets of gluten-free bread machine skill.

Through trial and error, endless experiments, and a dash of creativity, I slowly unraveled the mysteries of gluten-free bread baking. I found the unique properties of alternative flours like rice, sorghum, and quinoa. I learned the importance of xanthan gum and other binding agents in ensuring a pleasing texture. And with each successful loaf that emerged from my bread machine, my confidence soared, and my love for gluten-free baking grew.

The emotional transformation I experienced through gluten-free bread machine baking was remarkable. No longer confined to store-bought choices that often left much to be desired, I found freedom in the kitchen. I could finally indulge in freshly baked bread that fit my dietary needs and tantalized my taste buds. It was a revelation—a newfound culinary adventure that filled my life with joy and happiness.

Now, I stand before you, bursting with excitement to share my knowledge, tips, and recipes in this gluten-free bread machine cookbook. Within these pages, you will find a treasure trove of carefully curated recipes that accept the full spectrum of flavors and textures. From classic white bread to hearty multigrain loaves, from sweet indulgences to savory treats, this cookbook will guide you on a tantalizing journey that celebrates the art of gluten-free bread machine baking.

So, dear reader, I invite you to start on this culinary adventure with me. Embrace the burst of flavors, the perplexity of techniques, and the freedom that comes with learning gluten-free bread machine baking. Together, let us shatter the misconception that gluten-free bread cannot be delicious, and instead, savor the triumph of making mouthwatering loaves that will delight your senses and nourish your soul.

Welcome to the world of gluten-free bread machine baking—where flavor and freedom intertwine, and the options are as boundless as your imagination. Let's bake our way to a gluten-free heaven, one loaf at a time.

About Gluten Free Baking

Baking has always been my artistic outlet, a way to express myself through the alchemy of flour, sugar, and butter. But when gluten became my unsuspecting foe, my world of baking was turned upside down. Suddenly, the usual ingredients that brought me joy and comfort had to be reconsidered. I started on a gluten-free baking journey, a path filled with bursting flavors and perplexing challenges.

At first, the idea of gluten-free baking seemed like an insurmountable hurdle. How could I achieve the same textures and flavors without the magical binding powers of gluten? Doubt crept in, but my determination to continue following my passion burned brighter. Armed with a stack of gluten-free flours, a collection of recipes, and a heart full of hope, I dove deeply into the world of gluten-free baking.

The original attempts were met with mixed results. The breads were dense and lacked the usual springiness. The cookies collapsed at the slightest touch. But amidst the moments of frustration, there were bursts of flavor that surprised and thrilled my taste buds. I found the nutty richness of almond flour, the subtle sweetness of coconut flour, and the earthy complexity of buckwheat flour. Each ingredient brought its own unique burst of flavor, giving depth and character to my creations.

As I delved deeper into the realm of gluten-free baking, I met a myriad of perplexing challenges. The absence of gluten meant that I had to try with alternative binders and leavening agents. Xanthan gum became my secret weapon, adding elasticity and structure to breads and pastries. Baking powder and baking soda took on new importance, their exact measurements determining the rise and texture of my treats. It was a delicate dance of proportions and substitutions, a puzzle that needed patience and perseverance.

But with each challenge, there was a chance for growth and discovery. I learned to embrace the art of improvisation, adapting recipes and methods to suit the demands of gluten-free baking. I experimented with flaxseed meal as an egg substitute, found the magic of psyllium husk as a binding agent, and explored the wonders of aquafaba—a whipped chickpea liquid that mimicked the properties of egg whites. The kitchen became my laboratory, and I the mad scientist, concocting gluten-free treats that defied expectations.

Through the trials and tribulations, I discovered a newfound respect for the subtleties of flavor. Without the power of gluten, other ingredients had a chance to shine. The delicate sweetness of rice flour, the earthy nuttiness of teff flour, and the meaty richness of sorghum flour all took center stage. Each bite became a revelation—a burst of unexpected flavors that awakened my senses and challenged my ideas of what gluten-free baking could be.

Gluten-free baking has transformed from a daunting task into a profound source of joy and fulfillment. It has taught me resilience in the face of adversity and the power of embracing limits as catalysts for creativity. It has shown me that bursting flavors can emerge from unexpected places and that perplexing challenges can lead to the most rewarding victories.

So, to all those starting on their own gluten-free baking journey, I urge you to embrace the burstiness and perplexity that awaits. Embrace the flavors that will surprise and please you. Embrace the difficulties that will push you to new heights of ingenuity. And above all, accept the joy that comes from creating gluten-free baked goods that are a reflection of your unique spirit and unwavering determination.

Let us enjoy the art of gluten-free baking together, as we unlock the secrets of bursting flavors and navigate the perplexing world of gluten-free delights. With each creation, we defy expectations and redefine what it means to savor the simple joys of a homemade treat. So, my fellow gluten-free bakers, let us start on this journey of bursting flavors and perplexing delights, one recipe at a time.

Benefits of Using a Bread Machine

One of the most perplexing parts of bread making had been kneading the dough. The physical effort needed often left me exhausted and uncertain if I had achieved the right consistency. But with the touch of a button, the bread machine effortlessly took on the job. It kneaded the dough to perfection, allowing me to skip the laborious process and freeing up my time for other activities. The burst of relief I felt was matched only by the anticipation of the beauty that would emerge from the machine.

Another burst of joy came from the convenience of using a bread machine. The perplexing task of monitoring the dough's rise and ensuring the right temperature was a thing of the past. The machine provided the ideal environment for fermentation, with precise timing and temperature controls that gave consistent results. I could set it before bed and wake up to the heady aroma of freshly baked bread. It was a burst of convenience that changed my mornings and brought a sense of magic to my breakfast table.

Beyond the burstiness and joy, using a bread machine also offered me a newfound sense of freedom. Gluten-free baking, in particular, had previously been a perplexing task. Achieving the right texture and rise seemed like an impossible feat. But the bread machine became my ally in this journey, offering a controlled environment that allowed gluten-free dough to develop its full potential. It eliminated the guesswork and gave the burst of confidence I needed to experiment with new recipes and flavors.

The benefits of using a bread machine went beyond traditional breads. It became a versatile tool, allowing me to explore a world of culinary options. Sweet breads, pizza dough, cinnamon rolls—the choices were endless. With each burst of creativity, the bread machine was there to support my experiments, making the process seamless and pleasant.

The burst of joy I experienced from using a bread machine was not limited to the end product. It stretched to the entire baking experience. The machine became a source of inspiration, sparking my imagination and pushing me to try new techniques and flavor combinations. It breathed life into my kitchen, infusing it with the tantalizing scent of freshly baked bread and the sense of success that comes from making something with your own hands.

In my personal journey, the choice to embrace a bread machine has been transformative. It has brought great delight to my baking routine, elevating it to new heights. The convenience, consistency, and freedom it offers have rekindled my love for the craft and expanded the boundaries of what I thought was possible in the realm of homemade bread.

So, if you find yourself yearning for bursting flavors, seeking convenience, and craving the freedom to create, I highly suggest embracing the magic of a bread machine. Let it be your partner in the kitchen, your catalyst for culinary discovery. Embrace the burstiness and perplexity it brings, and watch as it changes your baking experience into a world of endless possibilities.

Understanding Gluten-Free Flours and Ingredients

As someone who loves the art of baking, I started on this adventure with bursting excitement, eager to create delectable treats that would rival their gluten-filled counterparts. Along the way, I found a treasure trove of tips and techniques that have paved the path to successful gluten-free baking. So, with a burst of enthusiasm, let me share my personal insights and tips to help you navigate the perplexities of this gluten-free world.

Embrace a Variety of Flours: The world of gluten-free flours is vast and bursting with unique tastes and textures. Experimenting with different flour blends is key to getting successful results. A perplexing combination that has worked wonders for me includes a mix of rice flour, almond flour, and tapioca flour. This blend provides a burst of lightness, while the almond flour adds a nutty richness that is truly delicious.

Add Binders and Stabilizers: Gluten is responsible for the elasticity and structure in traditional baking, so finding suitable replacements is vital. Xanthan gum or guar gum are popular binders that can help mimic the stretchiness of gluten. Start with small amounts and change as needed based on the recipe. This perplexing ingredient might seem intimidating, but it plays a vital role in getting the desired texture.

Pay Attention to Liquid Ratios: Gluten-free flours tend to absorb more liquid than their wheat counterparts, so it's important to adjust the liquid ratios in your recipes. This burst of knowledge will ensure your mixes and doughs have the right consistency. If a recipe seems too dry, don't fear to add a bit more liquid, whether it's water, milk, or another liquid suitable for the recipe.

Enhance Flavors with Add-ins: Gluten-free baking presents a burst of chances to get creative with add-ins and flavorings. Perplexing as it may seem, ingredients like dried fruits, nuts, chocolate chips, or even a burst of aromatic spices can turn your creations into something truly special. Add-ins not only enhance the taste but also provide textural interest, creating a truly personal touch.

Mindful Mixing and Leavening: Mixing techniques play a key role in gluten-free baking. Too much mixing can cause excessive air incorporation, resulting in a thick and gummy texture. A burst of patience is needed to achieve the perfect balance. Additionally, pay attention to leavening agents such as baking powder and baking soda. Gluten-free batters often benefit from an extra burst of leavening, so don't hesitate to change the quantities accordingly.

Let It Rest: After mixing your gluten-free dough or batter, let it rest for a short time. This perplexing step helps the flours to absorb the liquids fully, resulting in better texture and flavor. Patience is key here, as the resting time can vary based on the recipe and ingredients used.

Invest in Quality Baking Tools: Gluten-free baking takes precision, and having the right tools can make a world of difference. Invest in a good quality kitchen scale for exact measurements. A perplexing assortment of mixing bowls, non-stick pans, and silicone baking mats will also prove useful in your gluten-free baking adventures.

Temperature and Timing: Gluten-free mixes and doughs often benefit from slightly different baking temperatures and times. Keep a close eye on your creations as they bake, and rely on visual signs rather than strict timings. A burst of golden-brown color and a toothpick inserted into the center coming out clean are good signs of doneness.

Seek Support and Inspiration: The gluten-free baking community is bursting with helpful tools and perplexing insights. Join online forums or social media groups where you can connect with fellow bakers, share tips, and find inspiration. Sharing your successes and challenges with like-minded people can be an invaluable source of support on your gluten-free baking journey.

Embrace the Learning Process: Gluten-free baking is a continual learning process. Don't be discouraged by initial failures or perplexing results. Each baking endeavor brings new information and understanding. Embrace the burst of growth and remember that even the most experienced bakers face challenges along the way.

As I think on my personal gluten-free baking journey, I am filled with bursting gratitude for the lessons learned and the delicious creations that have emerged from my kitchen. The perplexities of gluten-free baking have pushed me to explore new flavors, try with different techniques, and unlock the secrets to successful gluten-free treats.

Let the secrets of successful gluten-free baking unleash your inner baker and open up a world of possibilities that will leave you bursting with joy.

Tips for Successful Gluten-Free Baking

Gluten-free baking has received significant attention in recent years, as more individuals are seeking alternatives to traditional wheat-based products. The world of gluten-free flours and ingredients can be perplexing, with a burst of options available, each with its unique traits and characteristics. As someone who has explored the intricacies of gluten-free baking, I have come to understand the importance of these ingredients and how they add to the texture, taste, and overall success of gluten-free creations. So, let's start on a journey of unraveling the mystery surrounding gluten-free flours and ingredients.

a. Rice Flour: Rice flour is one of the most widely used gluten-free flours. It comes in both white and brown varieties, and each offers a unique burst of flavor and texture. White rice flour has a milder taste and makes a lighter texture, making it ideal for cakes, pastries, and delicate baked goods. Brown rice flour has a nuttier flavor and a slightly denser texture, making it perfect for heartier breads and muffins. Experimenting with different ratios of white and brown rice flour can provide a burst of variety in your gluten-free baking.

b. Almond Flour: Almond flour is a puzzling ingredient that adds a burst of richness and moisture to gluten-free recipes. Made from finely ground almonds, it offers a delicate nutty flavor that goes well with a variety of sweet and savory recipes. Almond flour is often used in cakes, cookies, and pie crusts, as well as in gluten-free breads for extra moisture and tenderness. Its high fat content can add to a burst of denseness, so it's best to combine it with other flours or use it in conjunction with binders and stabilizers.

   c. *Coconut Flour*: Bursting onto the gluten-free scene with its unique properties, coconut flour has gained fame among bakers. Made from dried, ground coconut meat, it gives a distinct burst of flavor and a high fiber content. Coconut flour absorbs more liquid than other flours, so recipes often require a higher amount of liquid ingredients. It gives a light and fluffy texture to baked goods, making it suitable for cakes, muffins, and pancakes. However, its absorbent nature can also make it perplexing to work with, so it's best to follow recipes specifically designed for coconut flour or try with small amounts to achieve the desired results.

   d. *Tapioca Flour/Starch:* Tapioca flour, also known as tapioca starch, is a staple in gluten-free baking. It is made from the starchy removed from the cassava root and offers a burst of lightness and chewiness to baked goods. Tapioca flour is often used in combination with other gluten-free flours to improve texture and binding qualities. It adds a pleasant springiness to breads, cookies, and pizza crusts, making them more reminiscent of their wheat-based versions. Its neutral taste and fine texture make it a versatile ingredient in gluten-free recipes.

   e. *Potato Starch:* Potato starch is produced from peeled potatoes that are dried and ground into a fine powder. It is a popular choice for gluten-free baking due to its ability to add a burst of wetness and softness to baked goods. Potato starch is often used in combination with other flours to improve texture and increase the shelf life of gluten-free breads and desserts. It contributes to a tender crumb and helps retain moisture, which is especially beneficial in gluten-free cakes and cookies. However, it is important to note that potato starch differs from potato flour, which has a higher potato content and may give different results in recipes.

f. Sorghum Flour: Sorghum flour, made from the grain of the sorghum plant, is getting recognition as a versatile gluten-free flour. It offers a burst of earthy and slightly sweet flavors, making it perfect for a wide range of recipes. Sorghum flour works well in bread, muffin, and pancake recipes, giving a tender crumb and good structure. It can also be used as a substitute for wheat flour in savory recipes such as roux or as a coating for fried foods. Its unique taste profile adds depth to gluten-free creations and makes it a valuable addition to any gluten-free pantry.

g. Buckwheat Flour: Despite its name, buckwheat is not linked to wheat and is naturally gluten-free. Buckwheat flour, made from ground buckwheat groats, offers a burst of nutty flavor and a thick, hearty texture. It is often used in the making of gluten-free breads, pancakes, and soba noodles. Buckwheat flour can be mixed with other gluten-free flours to add complexity to baked goods or used on its own for a more distinct taste. Its rich nutritional profile, including high amounts of fiber and protein, makes it a popular choice for those seeking healthier gluten-free options.

h. Xanthan Gum and Guar Gum: Xanthan gum and guar gum are perplexing ingredients that serve as binders and supports in gluten-free baking. They mimic the properties of gluten, giving structure and elasticity to the final baked goods. Xanthan gum is produced from the fermentation of sugar by bacteria, while guar gum is extracted from the guar bean. Both gums are highly effective in small amounts, so it's important to use them sparingly to avoid a slimy or gummy texture. They are widely used in recipes that require a burst of structure, such as bread, pizza dough, and cakes. However, it's worth noting that some people may have sensitivities or allergies to these gums, so it's important to consider alternatives or omit them if necessary.

i. Alternative Sweeteners: In addition to flours and binders, sweeteners play a key role in gluten-free baking. Traditional white sugar can be used, but there is a burst of alternative sweeteners that offer unique tastes and health benefits. Perplexing choices like honey, maple syrup, agave nectar, and coconut sugar provide natural sweetness and can add depth to gluten-free treats. It's important to note that alternative sweeteners may affect the texture and moisture content of the finished product, so adjustments to the recipe may be necessary.

j. Egg Replacements: Flaxseed eggs are widely used in baking as a source of moisture, structure, and leavening. For those following a gluten-free and vegan lifestyle or have egg allergies, finding suitable replacements is vital. Perplexing as it may seem, there are several options offered. Common egg replacements include applesauce, mashed bananas, flaxseed or chia seed gel, soft tofu, and commercial egg replacers. Each of these alternatives offers a unique burst of texture and moisture, so experimentation may be needed to achieve the desired results.

Understanding the properties and characteristics of gluten-free flours and ingredients is important for successful baking. It allows you to make informed choices, tailor recipes to your tastes, and achieve the best possible results. Embrace the burst of versatility and creativity that gluten-free baking offers, and don't be afraid to try and adapt recipes to fit your needs. With time, practice, and a touch of perseverance, you'll find the secrets to creating delicious gluten-free treats that will leave everyone perplexed and amazed.

Gluten-Free Bread Basics

Bread has always been a source of comfort and joy for me. But when I found that I needed to follow a gluten-free diet, I felt a sense of perplexity and unease. How could I enjoy the simple pleasure of a warm, freshly baked loaf without the very ingredient that gives it shape and elasticity? Determined to find a solution, I went on a personal journey into the world of gluten-free bread basics, looking to recreate that burst of satisfaction I once knew.

The first perplexing challenge I met was flour selection. Gluten-free baking needs a different arsenal of flours to replace the wheat flour I was accustomed to. Rice flour, almond flour, and tapioca flour became my new friends in the kitchen. But a burst of flavor and texture escaped me. It was only when I began experimenting with different flour blends that I started to uncover the secrets. A combination of rice flour, sorghum flour, and potato starch produced a burst of complexity that mimicked the texture of traditional bread. Each flour brought its own unique perplexity to the mix, and the blend became my hidden weapon.

Binders and stabilizers were another perplexing feature of gluten-free bread. Gluten acts as a glue in traditional bread, holding everything together. In its absence, I needed to find options. Xanthan gum and guar gum, both perplexing substances at first, proved to be essential. These binders provided the much-needed elasticity and cohesion in the dough, preventing it from crumbling into a disappointing mess. As I experimented with different ratios, the burst of success became more obvious. The dough held together, and the resulting loaves had a pleasant springiness that I had thought was lost to me forever.

Leavening agents offered another burst of perplexity. Yeast, the go-to leavening agent in traditional bread, was not a choice for me. Baking powder and baking soda came to the rescue. As I watched them react with moisture and heat, releasing carbon dioxide gas, I witnessed the burst of rise that I wished for. But it wasn't just the leavening agents alone. A touch of vinegar or lemon juice gave a perplexing twist to the process, enhancing the rise and improving the texture of the bread. It was a burst of chemistry that turned the dough into something magical.

The moisture level of gluten-free bread was a perplexing puzzle in itself. Gluten-free flours have a tendency to absorb more liquid than their wheat cousins. Finding the right balance was important. Too much wetness resulted in a soggy mess, while too little left the bread dry and crumbly. It took trial and error, a burst of patience, and careful attention to achieve the right balance. Following the directions in the recipe became my guiding light, and making adjustments became second nature. The burst of pleasure came when I finally achieved a moist, tender crumb that rivalled traditional bread.

Mixing and kneading were yet another perplexing part of gluten-free bread making. Kneading, which creates gluten strands in traditional bread, was less important here. Instead, I worked on achieving a well-mixed and evenly distributed dough. Overmixing became my enemy, as it resulted in a dense and gummy texture. I learned to mix until just mixed, allowing the ingredients to come together without overworking them. Resting or proofing the dough became a valuable burst of time, allowing the flavors to form and the dough to hydrate. The result was a burst of improved texture and taste in the end bread.

Baking skills took on a perplexing twist in the world of gluten-free bread. Traditional bread needs a high temperature to achieve a golden crust and a fully cooked interior. But gluten-free bread required a different approach. Baking at a lower temperature for a longer time became my secret tool. This ensured that the bread cooked evenly, avoiding excessive browning on the outside while staying undercooked on the inside. Covering the bread with foil during the latter part of baking stopped that burst of disappointment. It was a perplexing dance of time and temperature that ended in a burst of perfectly baked gluten-free loaves.

Once the bread came from the machine, a burst of anticipation filled the air. But I had to practice patience and allow it to cool completely before slicing. Gluten-free bread, I found, is more delicate and crumblier when warm. Cooling allowed it to set and hold its shape, making a burst of sliceable perfection. Storing it properly, in an airtight jar or bag, ensured its freshness. But I soon learned that gluten-free bread has a shorter shelf life than traditional bread. It was a perplexing discovery, but I found solace in freezing the bread for longer storage. Slicing it before freezing and separating each slice with parchment paper allowed for an easy thaw and a burst of ease.

My personal journey into gluten-free bread basics has been a burst of perplexity and success. From choosing the right flour blend to experimenting with binders, leavening agents, and moisture ratios, each step has brought its own challenges and moments of revelation. It has been a journey of trial and error, of accepting the perplexing nature of gluten-free baking, and finding bursts of success along the way.

But beyond the technicalities, this journey has been highly personal. It has taught me patience and resolve. It has made me enjoy the simple pleasure of a warm slice of bread even more. And it has given me a burst of creativity in the kitchen, as I continue to play with flavors, add-ins, and different bread recipes.

Gluten-free bread basics may seem confusing at first, but with time and practice, it becomes an art form. It's about understanding the ingredients, listening to the dough, and adapting to the unique challenges that gluten-free baking offers. It's about finding the burst of satisfaction in making something delicious that nourishes both the body and the soul.

To all those starting on their own gluten-free bread journey, embrace the perplexity and allow yourself to be captivated by the bursts of triumph. Discover the joy of making a loaf that brings comfort and nourishment to your gluten-free lifestyle. And remember, in every slice, there is a burst of possibility waiting to be enjoyed.

Essential Equipment and Ingredients

For those following a gluten-free diet, the quest for a perfect loaf of bread can be difficult. The absence of gluten, the protein responsible for the elasticity and structure of traditional bread, requires a different method to achieve that desired texture and taste. Enter the gluten-free bread machine—a useful tool that simplifies the process and produces delicious loaves with ease. In this article, we will explore the essential equipment and ingredients needed to make gluten-free bread machine magic.

Gluten-Free Bread Machine

The first and most important piece of equipment is, of course, the gluten-free bread machine itself. These appliances are specifically made to accommodate the unique requirements of gluten-free bread baking. When selecting a machine, there are a few key factors to consider:

a. Customizable Settings: Look for a bread machine that offers customizable settings, such as a gluten-free cycle or a programmable choice. This allows you to tailor the baking process to fit your specific recipe and preferences.

b. Loaf Size Options: Consider the loaf size options offered. Gluten-free bread tends to be thicker and may require a smaller loaf size to ensure even baking.

c. Mixing and Kneading Paddles: Check if the machine comes with detachable paddles. Since gluten-free bread requires a gentler mixing and kneading process, having the ability to remove the paddles after the initial mixing phase helps to prevent excessive air incorporation and give a better texture.

Gluten-Free Bread Mixes

Gluten-free bread mixes are a convenient choice for beginners or those who prefer a hassle-free baking experience. These mixes typically contain a blend of gluten-free flours and other important ingredients, such as binders and stabilizers. They offer a reliable base for your bread machine experiments and save you the trouble of finding individual ingredients. Look for reputable brands that offer a variety of flavors and textures to fit your preferences.

Gluten-Free Flour Blends

If you prefer a more hands-on approach or want to experiment with different flavors and textures, creating your own gluten-free flour blend is a great choice. Building a blend allows you to customize the taste and texture of your bread to fit your preferences. Some common gluten-free flours and starches that can be used in a blend include:

a. Rice Flour: Rice flour is a useful gluten-free flour that provides a neutral taste and helps create a light and fluffy texture.

b. Sorghum Flour: Sorghum flour adds a slightly sweet and nutty flavor to the bread while enhancing the general structure.

c. Potato Starch: Potato starch adds to the softness and moisture retention of the bread.

d. Tapioca Starch: Tapioca starch, also known as tapioca flour, adds chewiness and flexibility to the bread.

e. Almond Flour: Almond flour brings a delicate nuttiness to the bread and adds wetness.

Binders and Stabilizers

In the absence of gluten, binders and stabilizers are necessary to provide structure and cohesion to the bread dough. These ingredients prevent the bread from becoming crumbly or falling apart. Common binders and preservatives used in gluten-free bread baking include:

a. Xanthan Gum: Xanthan gum is a natural thickening and binding agent that helps mimic the flexibility of gluten. It improves the taste and structure of the bread.

b. Guar Gum: Guar gum is another natural thickening and binding agent that helps hold the ingredients together and stops crumbling.

The proper amount of binders and stabilizers will depend on your specific recipe, so be sure to follow the instructions given.

Leavening Agents

Leavening agents are important for achieving the desired rise and lightness in gluten-free bread. While yeast is usually used in bread baking, gluten-free bread often relies on alternative leavening agents that work well in the absence of gluten. Two common choices are:

a. Baking Powder: Baking powder is a mixture of baking soda, cream of tartar, and a moisture-activated acid. It produces carbon dioxide gas when heated, resulting in a rise in the bread.

b. Baking Soda: Baking soda, when combined with an acid, such as vinegar or lemon juice, makes carbon dioxide gas and helps the bread to rise.

Ensure that your leavening agents are fresh and active for optimal effects.

Other Ingredients

In addition to the necessary equipment and ingredients listed above, you may want to consider incorporating other ingredients to enhance the flavor and texture of your gluten-free bread. Some popular choices include:

a. Flaxseed eggs*:* Flaxseed eggs provide moisture, structure, and binding abilities. They also add to the richness and tenderness of the bread.

b. Sweeteners: Sweeteners like honey, maple syrup, or sugar add a touch of sweetness and help with cooking. They can also improve the overall flavor profile of your bread.

c. Fats: Fats, such as veggie oil or melted butter, add moisture and tenderness to the bread.

d. Salt: Salt not only enhances the flavor of the bread but also helps control the fermentation process and improve the texture.

e. Flavorings and Add-Ins: Get creative with your gluten-free bread by adding flavorings and add-ins such as herbs, spices, dried fruits, nuts, or seeds. These items can add bursts of flavor and texture to your loaves.

Hydration and Moisture

Proper hydration and moisture are important for achieving the desired texture in gluten-free bread. Gluten-free flours tend to absorb more liquid than wheat flour, so it's important to adjust the liquid content properly. Too little moisture can result in dry and crumbly bread, while too much can lead to a dense and gummy structure. It's suggested to follow the recipe instructions regarding the liquid-to-flour ratio and adjust it as needed to achieve the desired texture. Additionally, adding ingredients like Flaxseed eggs, yogurt, or applesauce can help add moisture to the bread.

Mixing and Kneading Techniques

The mixing and kneading process for gluten-free bread varies from traditional bread. Gluten-free bread dough requires less vigorous mixing to avoid excess air incorporation, which can result in a dense texture. Gentle mixing is usually recommended to ensure an even distribution of ingredients without overworking the dough. Some gluten-free bread recipes may call for extra mixing or resting time to allow the flour to fully hydrate and develop its structure. It's important to follow the exact instructions in your recipe to achieve the best results.

Baking Techniques

Baking methods play a significant role in achieving the desired texture and structure in gluten-free bread. Heating the bread machine is important to ensure proper heat distribution and even baking. It's important to follow the recommended baking temperature and time stated in the recipe to achieve optimal results. Overbaking gluten-free bread can result in a dry and crumbly texture, so it's important to watch the bread closely during the baking process.

Cooling and Storing

Proper cooling and storing techniques are important for maintaining the texture of gluten-free bread. Gluten-free bread tends to be more fragile when warm, so it's important to allow it to cool fully before slicing. After cooling, store the bread in an airtight container or bag to preserve moisture and prevent it from drying out. Gluten-free bread is best eaten within a few days or can be frozen for longer storage.

Knowing the factors that influence gluten-free bread texture and structure is key to achieving successful results. The selection of gluten-free flours, binding agents, leavening agents, and proper hydration and moisture, along with appropriate mixing and kneading techniques, baking methods, and cooling and storing practices all add to the final texture and structure of gluten-free bread. It may take some experimentation and adjustments to find the right combination for your desired results. With practice and attention to these factors, you can make delicious gluten-free bread that rivals its gluten-containing counterparts. Enjoy the process and enjoy the satisfaction of baking gluten-free bread with a delightful texture and structure.

Remember to follow your specific recipe for ingredient measurements and instructions, as the ratios may change depending on the intended outcome.

A gluten-free bread machine, along with the necessary equipment and ingredients, is a valuable asset in your quest for delicious gluten-free bread. Whether you opt for convenient bread mixes or make your own flour blends, the key is to experiment, adjust, and customize based on your preferences. With the right mix of equipment and ingredients, you can achieve a burst of satisfaction with each gluten-free loaf that emerges from your bread machine. So, unleash your creativity, accept the gluten-free journey, and enjoy the delightful world of gluten-free bread baking.

Tips for Achieving the Best Results in a Bread Machine

Bread machines have changed the process of making homemade bread. Whether you're a beginner or an experienced baker, using a bread machine can simplify the bread-making process and give delicious results. In this piece, we will provide you with valuable tips to help you achieve the best results when using a bread machine.

Read the Manual

Before you start using your bread machine, it's important to read the instruction manual thoroughly. Each bread machine model may have unique requirements and features that you need to be aware of. Familiarize yourself with the machine's settings, instructions for adding ingredients, and suggested bread recipes. Understanding your bread machine's capabilities and limits will help you achieve optimal results.

Measure Ingredients Accurately

Accurate measurement of ingredients is important for successful bread machine baking. Use measuring cups and spoons especially designed for dry and liquid ingredients. Level off dry ingredients, such as flour, with a straight edge to ensure accuracy. Be precise when measuring yeast, salt, sugar, and other ingredients as stated in the recipe. Inaccurate measures can impact the bread's texture and rise.

Follow the Recommended Order of Ingredients

Most bread machine manufacturers suggest a specific order for adding ingredients to the machine's pan. Typically, the order is as follows: wet ingredients first (water, milk, Flaxseed eggs), followed by dry ingredients (flour, sugar, salt), and finally, the yeast. Adding ingredients in the correct order enables proper mixing and activation of the yeast at the appropriate time.

Use the Right Flour

Choosing the right flour is crucial for getting good results in a bread machine. While all-purpose flour is widely used, you can experiment with different types of flour, such as bread flour, whole wheat flour, or even gluten-free flour. Each type of flour has its own characteristics, and the results may change. It's important to follow recipes that specify the proper type of flour to achieve the desired texture and flavor.

Measure Water Carefully

The amount of water used in bread machine recipes is crucial for getting the right consistency of the dough. Too little water can result in a dry and thick loaf, while too much water can lead to a collapsed or soggy bread. Use a measuring cup specifically made for liquids and measure the water at eye level to ensure accuracy.

Experiment with Different Recipes

Don't be afraid to try with different bread recipes in your machine. Most bread machines come with a range of recipes to try, or you can find numerous recipes online. Start with basic recipes and gradually discover more complex ones. Follow the instructions carefully and note any adjustments you may need to make based on the unique characteristics of your machine.

Understand the Settings

Become familiar with the settings and choices available on your bread machine. Common options include basic, rapid, whole wheat, dough, and gluten-free. Each setting has specific guidelines for kneading, rising, and baking. Understand the differences between these settings and choose the one that best fits your recipe and desired results.

Experiment with Delayed Start

One of the advantages of a bread machine is the ability to use the delayed start option. This allows you to add ingredients to the machine, set the desired start time, and wake up or return home to freshly baked bread. Experiment with this feature, but keep in mind that ingredients like milk, Flaxseed eggs, and other perishable items should be used carefully when using a delayed start.

Monitor the Dough

During the kneading cycle, notice the dough's consistency. The dough should make a smooth ball and pull away cleanly from the sides of the pan. If the dough looks too dry or too wet, you may need to adjust the recipe by adding a little more water or flour. Monitoring the dough's consistency will help you troubleshoot any issues and make changes for better results.

Maintain the Machine

Regular maintenance of your bread machine is important for its longevity and best performance. Follow the manufacturer's directions for cleaning and maintaining the machine. Remove the pan and paddle after each use and clean them thoroughly. Keep the machine's surface clean and free from any spills or residue. Regular maintenance ensures that your machine works efficiently and consistently makes excellent bread.

Enjoy Freshly Baked Bread

Once the bread is done baking, carefully take it from the pan using mitts or silicone gloves. Allow the bread to cool on a wire rack before slicing. This helps to keep the bread's structure and prevents it from becoming gummy. Enjoy the delightful aroma and taste of homemade bread, and be proud of your baking successes!

Using a bread machine can be a rewarding and easy way to bake fresh bread at home. By following these tips, you can achieve the best results in your bread machine. Remember to read the manual, measure ingredients correctly, follow the recommended order of ingredients, and experiment with different recipes. Understand the settings on your machine, watch the dough's consistency, and maintain the machine regularly. With practice and experience, you will become more comfortable and confident in using your bread machine to make delicious homemade bread. So, roll up your sleeves, gather your ingredients, and let your bread machine work its magic. Enjoy the process and enjoy the satisfaction of baking your own bread!

Part 2

Special Bread Recipes

1. Herb and Olive Oil Bread

Ingredients:
- 2 cups gluten-free all-purpose flour
- 1 1/2 teaspoons xanthan gum
- 1 tablespoon sugar
- 1 teaspoon salt
- Use 1 packet (2 1/4 teaspoons) of active dry yeast.
- 1 cup warm water
- 1/4 cup olive oil
- 2 flaxseed eggs (2 tablespoons ground flaxseed + 6 tablespoons water)
- 1 tablespoon mixed dried herbs (rosemary, thyme, oregano)

Preparation Time:

Total: 2 hours (including rise time)

Instructions:

- *Prepare Flaxseed eggs:*
- In a small bowl, mix 2 tablespoons of ground flaxseed with 6 tablespoons of water. Allow the yeast to sit for a few minutes until it thickens and forms a gel-like consistency.
- *Prepare the Yeast Mixture:*
- Combine warm water, sugar, and yeast in the bread machine pan. Allow the mixture to sit for 5-10 minutes until it develops a frothy texture.
- *Add Wet Ingredients:*
- Pour olive oil into the yeast mixture in the bread machine.
- *Prepare Dry Ingredients:*
- In a separate bowl, whisk together gluten-free flour, xanthan gum, salt, and mixed dried herbs.
- *Combine Ingredients in the Bread Machine:*
- Add the dry ingredients to the bread machine pan over the wet ingredients.
- *Create a Well for Yeast:*
- Make a small well in the center of the dry ingredients and add the yeast.
- *Add Flaxseed eggs:*
- Pour the prepared flaxseed eggs into the bread machine pan.
- *Set the Bread Machine:*
- Select the gluten-free setting on the bread machine and begin the cycle.
- *Let the Bread Machine Work:*
- Allow the bread machine to complete the cycle. It will mix, knead, and rise the dough.
- *Final Rise and Bake:*

- Once the mixing and rising cycles are complete, leave the dough in the machine for an additional 30 minutes for the final rise and bake.

Nutritional Values (per slice):

- Calories: 120
- Protein: 2g
- Fat: 5g
- Carbs: 18g
- Fiber: 1g
- Sugars: 1g

Yield:

Approximately 12 slices

Enjoy:

- Once the baking is complete, carefully remove the gluten-free herb and olive oil bread from the machine, and let it cool on a wire rack before slicing.

Ingredients:

- 2 cups gluten-free all-purpose flour
- 1 1/2 teaspoons xanthan gum
- 1/4 cup sugar
- 1 teaspoon salt
- Use 1 packet (2 1/4 teaspoons) of active dry yeast.
- 1 cup warm almond milk
- 1/4 cup melted coconut oil
- 2 flaxseed eggs (2 tablespoons ground flaxseed + 6 tablespoons water)
- 1 teaspoon ground cinnamon
- 1/2 cup raisins

Preparation Time:

Total: 2 hours (including rise time)

Instructions:

- ***Prepare Flaxseed eggs:***
- In a small bowl, mix 2 tablespoons of ground flaxseed with 6 tablespoons of water. Allow the yeast to sit for a

few minutes until it thickens and forms a gel-like consistency.

- ***Prepare the Yeast Mixture:***
- In the bread machine pan, combine warm almond milk, sugar, and yeast. Let the yeast mixture rest for 5-10 minutes until it froths up.
- ***Add Wet Ingredients:***
- Pour melted coconut oil into the yeast mixture in the bread machine.
- ***Prepare Dry Ingredients:***
- In a separate bowl, whisk together gluten-free flour, xanthan gum, salt, and ground cinnamon.
- ***Combine Ingredients in the Bread Machine:***
- Add the dry ingredients to the bread machine pan over the wet ingredients.
- ***Create a Well for Yeast:***
- Make a small well in the center of the dry ingredients and add the yeast.
- ***Add Flaxseed eggs:***
- Pour the prepared flaxseed eggs into the bread machine pan.
- ***Set the Bread Machine:***
- Select the gluten-free setting on the bread machine and begin the cycle.
- ***Add Raisins:***
- Once the bread machine signals that it's time to add additional ingredients (usually after the initial mixing), add the raisins.
- ***Let the Bread Machine Work:***
- Allow the bread machine to complete the cycle. It will mix, knead, and rise the dough.
- ***Final Rise and Bake:***

- Once the mixing and rising cycles are complete, leave the dough in the machine for an additional 30 minutes for the final rise and bake.

Nutritional Values (per slice):

- Calories: 130
- Protein: 2g
- Fat: 6g
- Carbs: 18g
- Fiber: 1g
- Sugars: 5g

Yield:

Approximately 12 slices

- *Enjoy:*
- Once the baking is complete, carefully remove the gluten-free cinnamon raisin bread from the machine, and let it cool on a wire rack before slicing.

3. Sunflower Seed and Quinoa Bread

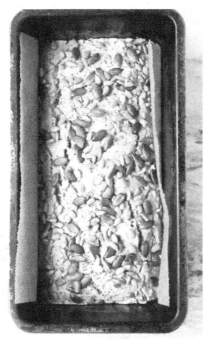

Ingredients:

- 1 1/2 cups gluten-free all-purpose flour
- 1 1/2 cups quinoa flour
- 1 1/2 teaspoons xanthan gum
- 1 tablespoon sugar
- 1 teaspoon salt
- Use 1 packet (2 1/4 teaspoons) of active dry yeast.
- 1 1/4 cups warm water
- 1/4 cup olive oil
- 2 flaxseed eggs (2 tablespoons ground flaxseed + 6 tablespoons water)
- 1/2 cup sunflower seeds

Preparation Time:

Total: 2 hours 30 minutes (including rise time)

Instructions:

- *Prepare Flaxseed eggs:*
- In a small bowl, mix 2 tablespoons of ground flaxseed with 6 tablespoons of water. Allow the yeast to sit for a few minutes until it thickens and forms a gel-like consistency.
- *Prepare the Yeast Mixture:*
- Combine warm water, sugar, and yeast in the bread machine pan. Allow the mixture to sit for 5-10 minutes until it develops a frothy texture.
- *Add Wet Ingredients:*
- Pour olive oil into the yeast mixture in the bread machine.
- *Prepare Dry Ingredients:*
- In a bowl, whisk together gluten-free all-purpose flour, quinoa flour, xanthan gum, and salt.
- *Combine Ingredients in the Bread Machine:*
- Add the dry ingredients to the bread machine pan over the wet ingredients.
- *Create a Well for Yeast:*
- Make a small well in the center of the dry ingredients and add the yeast.
- *Add Flaxseed eggs:*
- Pour the prepared flaxseed eggs into the bread machine pan.
- *Set the Bread Machine:*
- Select the gluten-free setting on the bread machine and begin the cycle.
- *Add Sunflower Seeds:*
- Once the bread machine signals that it's time to add additional ingredients (usually after the initial mixing), add the sunflower seeds.
- *Let the Bread Machine Work:*

- Allow the bread machine to complete the cycle. It will mix, knead, and rise the dough.
- ***Final Rise and Bake:***
- Once the mixing and rising cycles are complete, leave the dough in the machine for an additional 30 minutes for the final rise and bake.

Nutritional Values (per slice):
- Calories: 140
- Protein: 3g
- Fat: 7g
- Carbs: 16g
- Fiber: 2g
- Sugars: 1g

Yield:
- Approximately 12 slices

Enjoy:
- Once the baking is complete, carefully remove the gluten-free sunflower seed and quinoa bread from the machine, and let it cool on a wire rack before slicing.

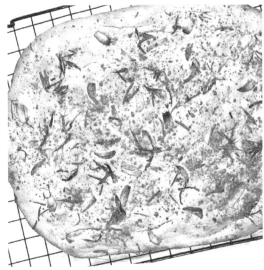

Ingredients:

- 2 1/2 cups gluten-free all-purpose flour
- 2 teaspoons xanthan gum
- 1 tablespoon sugar
- 1 teaspoon salt
- Use 1 packet (2 1/4 teaspoons) of active dry yeast.
- 1 cup warm water
- 1/4 cup olive oil
- 2 flaxseed eggs (2 tablespoons ground flaxseed + 6 tablespoons water)
- 2 tablespoons fresh rosemary, chopped
- 3 cloves garlic, minced

Preparation Time:

Total: 2 hours 15 minutes (including rise time)

Instructions:

- ***Prepare Flaxseed eggs:***

- In a small bowl, mix 2 tablespoons of ground flaxseed with 6 tablespoons of water. Let it sit for a few minutes until it thickens and forms a gel-like consistency.
- ***Prepare the Yeast Mixture:***
- Combine warm water, sugar, and yeast in the bread machine pan. Allow the mixture to sit for 5-10 minutes until it develops a frothy texture.
- ***Add Wet Ingredients:***
- Pour olive oil into the yeast mixture in the bread machine.
- ***Prepare Dry Ingredients:***
- In a bowl, whisk together gluten-free all-purpose flour, xanthan gum, salt, fresh rosemary, and minced garlic.
- ***Combine Ingredients in the Bread Machine:***
- Add the dry ingredients to the bread machine pan over the wet ingredients.
- ***Create a Well for Yeast:***
- Make a small well in the center of the dry ingredients and add the yeast.
- ***Add Flaxseed eggs:***
- Pour the prepared flaxseed eggs into the bread machine pan.
- ***Set the Bread Machine:***
- Select the gluten-free setting on the bread machine and begin the cycle.
- ***Let the Bread Machine Work:***
- Allow the bread machine to complete the cycle. It will mix, knead, and rise the dough.
- ***Final Rise and Bake:***
- Once the mixing and rising cycles are complete, leave the dough in the machine for an additional 30 minutes for the final rise and bake.

Nutritional Values (per slice):

- Calories: 150
- Protein: 3g
- Fat: 8g
- Carbs: 17g
- Fiber: 2g
- Sugars: 1g

Yield:

Approximately 12 slices

Enjoy:

- Once the baking is complete, carefully remove the gluten-free rosemary and garlic focaccia from the machine, and let it cool on a wire rack before slicing.

5. Cranberry Orange Loaf

Ingredients:

- 2 cups gluten-free all-purpose flour
- 1 1/2 teaspoons xanthan gum
- 1/2 cup sugar
- 1 teaspoon salt
- Use 1 packet (2 1/4 teaspoons) of active dry yeast.
- 1 cup warm orange juice
- 1/4 cup melted coconut oil
- 2 flaxseed eggs (2 tablespoons ground flaxseed + 6 tablespoons water)
- 1 cup dried cranberries

Preparation Time:

Total: 2 hours 30 minutes (including rise time)

Instructions:

- ***Prepare Flaxseed eggs:***
- In a small bowl, mix 2 tablespoons of ground flaxseed with 6 tablespoons of water. Let it sit for a few minutes until it thickens and forms a gel-like consistency.
- ***Prepare the Yeast Mixture:***

- In the bread machine pan, combine warm orange juice, sugar, and yeast. Allow the mixture to sit for 5-10 minutes until it develops a frothy texture.
- *Add Wet Ingredients:*
- Pour melted coconut oil into the yeast mixture in the bread machine.
- *Prepare Dry Ingredients:*
- In a bowl, whisk together gluten-free all-purpose flour, xanthan gum, salt.
- *Combine Ingredients in the Bread Machine:*
- Add the dry ingredients to the bread machine pan over the wet ingredients.
- *Create a Well for Yeast:*
- Make a small well in the center of the dry ingredients and add the yeast.
- *Add Flaxseed eggs:*
- Pour the prepared flaxseed eggs into the bread machine pan.
- *Set the Bread Machine:*
- Select the gluten-free setting on the bread machine and begin the cycle.
- *Add Cranberries*:
- Once the bread machine signals that it's time to add additional ingredients (usually after the initial mixing), add the dried cranberries.
- *Let the Bread Machine Work:*
- Allow the bread machine to complete the cycle. It will mix, knead, and rise the dough.
- *Final Rise and Bake:*
- Once the mixing and rising cycles are complete, leave the dough in the machine for an additional 30 minutes for the final rise and bake.

Nutritional Values (per slice):

- Calories: 160
- Protein: 2g
- Fat: 6g
- Carbs: 25g
- Fiber: 2g
- Sugars: 12g

Yield:

Approximately 12 slices

Enjoy:

- Once the baking is complete, carefully remove the gluten-free cranberry orange loaf from the machine, and let it cool on a wire rack before slicing.

6. Maple Pecan Bread

Ingredients:
- 2 cups gluten-free all-purpose flour
- 1 1/2 teaspoons xanthan gum
- 1/3 cup brown sugar
- 1 teaspoon salt
- Use 1 packet (2 1/4 teaspoons) of active dry yeast.
- 1 cup warm almond milk
- 1/4 cup melted coconut oil
- 2 flaxseed eggs (2 tablespoons ground flaxseed + 6 tablespoons water)
- 1/2 cup chopped pecans
- 2 tablespoons pure maple syrup

Preparation Time:
Total: 2 hours 30 minutes (including rise time)

Instructions:
- ***Prepare Flaxseed eggs:***
- In a small bowl, mix 2 tablespoons of ground flaxseed with 6 tablespoons of water. Let it sit for a few minutes until it thickens and forms a gel-like consistency.
- ***Prepare the Yeast Mixture:***

- In the bread machine pan, combine warm almond milk, brown sugar, and yeast. Allow the mixture to sit for 5-10 minutes until it develops a frothy texture.
- *Add Wet Ingredients:*
- Pour melted coconut oil into the yeast mixture in the bread machine.
- *Prepare Dry Ingredients:*
- In a bowl, whisk together gluten-free all-purpose flour, xanthan gum, salt.
- *Combine Ingredients in the Bread Machine:*
- Add the dry ingredients to the bread machine pan over the wet ingredients.
- *Create a Well for Yeast:*
- Make a small well in the center of the dry ingredients and add the yeast.
- *Add Flaxseed eggs:*
- Pour the prepared flaxseed eggs into the bread machine pan.
- *Set the Bread Machine:*
- Select the gluten-free setting on the bread machine and begin the cycle.
- **Add Pecans and Maple Syrup:**
- Once the bread machine signals that it's time to add additional ingredients (usually after the initial mixing), add the chopped pecans and drizzle in the maple syrup.
- *Let the Bread Machine Work:*
- Allow the bread machine to complete the cycle. It will mix, knead, and rise the dough.
- *Final Rise and Bake:*
- Once the mixing and rising cycles are complete, leave the dough in the machine for an additional 30 minutes for the final rise and bake.

Nutritional Values (per slice):

- Calories: 180
- Protein: 3g
- Fat: 9g
- Carbs: 23g
- Fiber: 2g
- Sugars: 8g

Yield:

Approximately 12 slices

Enjoy:

- Once the baking is complete, carefully remove the gluten-free maple pecan bread from the machine, and let it cool on a wire rack before slicing.

7. Seeded Multigrain Bread

Ingredients:
- 1 1/2 cups gluten-free all-purpose flour
- 1 cup quinoa flour
- 1/2 cup almond flour
- 1 1/2 teaspoons xanthan gum
- 1 tablespoon honey
- 1 teaspoon salt
- Use 1 packet (2 1/4 teaspoons) of active dry yeast.
- 1 1/4 cups warm water
- 1/4 cup olive oil
- 2 flaxseed eggs (2 tablespoons ground flaxseed + 6 tablespoons water)
- 1/4 cup sunflower seeds
- 1/4 cup pumpkin seeds
- 2 tablespoons chia seeds

Preparation Time:
Total: 3 hours (including rise time)

Instructions:
- ***Prepare Flaxseed eggs:***
- In a small bowl, mix 2 tablespoons of ground flaxseed with 6 tablespoons of water. Allow the yeast to sit for a few minutes until it thickens and forms a gel-like consistency.

- *Prepare the Yeast Mixture:*
- In the bread machine pan, combine warm water, honey, and yeast. Let the yeast mixture rest for 5-10 minutes until it froths up.
- *Add Wet Ingredients:*
- Pour olive oil into the yeast mixture in the bread machine.
- *Prepare Dry Ingredients:*
- In a bowl, whisk together gluten-free all-purpose flour, quinoa flour, almond flour, xanthan gum, and salt.
- *Combine Ingredients in the Bread Machine:*
- Add the dry ingredients to the bread machine pan over the wet ingredients.
- *Create a Well for Yeast:*
- Make a small well in the center of the dry ingredients and add the yeast.
- *Add Flaxseed eggs:*
- Pour the prepared Flaxseed eggs into the bread machine pan.
- *Set the Bread Machine:*
- Select the gluten-free setting on the bread machine and begin the cycle.
- **Add Seeds:**
- Once the bread machine signals that it's time to add additional ingredients (usually after the initial mixing), add the sunflower seeds, pumpkin seeds, and chia seeds.
- *Let the Bread Machine Work:*
- Allow the bread machine to complete the cycle. It will mix, knead, and rise the dough.
- *Final Rise and Bake:*
- Once the mixing and rising cycles are complete, leave the dough in the machine for an additional 30 minutes for the final rise and bake.

Nutritional Values (per slice):

- Calories: 160
- Protein: 4g
- Fat: 8g
- Carbs: 20g
- Fiber: 3g
- Sugars: 2g

<u>Yield:</u>

Approximately 12 slices

Enjoy:

- Once the baking is complete, carefully remove the gluten-free seeded multigrain bread from the machine, and let it cool on a wire rack before slicing.

Ingredients:

- 2 cups gluten-free all-purpose flour
- 1 1/2 teaspoons xanthan gum
- 1/2 cup sugar
- Zest of 2 lemons
- 1 teaspoon salt
- Use 1 packet (2 1/4 teaspoons) of active dry yeast.
- 1 cup warm almond milk
- 1/4 cup melted coconut oil
- 2 Flaxseed eggs (2 tablespoons ground flaxseed + 6 tablespoons water)
- 2 tablespoons poppy seeds
- Juice of 1 lemon

Preparation Time:

Total: 2 hours 30 minutes (including rise time)

Instructions:

- *Prepare Flaxseed eggs:*
- In a small bowl, mix 2 tablespoons of ground flaxseed with 6 tablespoons of water. Allow the yeast to sit for a few minutes until it thickens and forms a gel-like consistency.
- *Prepare the Yeast Mixture:*
- In the bread machine pan, combine warm almond milk, sugar, lemon zest, and yeast. Let the yeast mixture rest for 5-10 minutes until it froths up.
- *Add Wet Ingredients:*
- Pour melted coconut oil into the yeast mixture in the bread machine.
- *Prepare Dry Ingredients:*
- In a bowl, whisk together gluten-free all-purpose flour, xanthan gum, salt, and poppy seeds.
- *Combine Ingredients in the Bread Machine:*
- Add the dry ingredients to the bread machine pan over the wet ingredients.
- *Create a Well for Yeast:*
- Make a small well in the center of the dry ingredients and add the yeast.
- *Add Flaxseed eggs:*
- Pour the prepared Flaxseed eggs into the bread machine pan.
- *Set the Bread Machine:*
- Select the gluten-free setting on the bread machine and begin the cycle.
- *Add Lemon Juice:*
- Once the bread machine signals that it's time to add additional ingredients (usually after the initial mixing), add the juice of 1 lemon.
- *Let the Bread Machine Work:*

- Allow the bread machine to complete the cycle. It will mix, knead, and rise the dough.
- ***Final Rise and Bake:***
- Once the mixing and rising cycles are complete, leave the dough in the machine for an additional 30 minutes for the final rise and bake.

Nutritional Values (per slice):

- Calories: 150
- Protein: 2g
- Fat: 7g
- Carbs: 20g
- Fiber: 2g
- Sugars: 6g

Yield:

Approximately 12 slices

Enjoy:

- Once the baking is complete, carefully remove the gluten-free lemon poppy seed bread from the machine, and let it cool on a wire rack before slicing.

9. Chocolate Hazelnut Swirl Bread

Ingredients:
- 2 cups gluten-free all-purpose flour
- 1 1/2 teaspoons xanthan gum
- 1/3 cup cocoa powder
- 1/2 cup sugar
- 1 teaspoon salt
- Use 1 packet (2 1/4 teaspoons) of active dry yeast.
- 1 cup warm almond milk
- 1/4 cup melted coconut oil
- 2 Flaxseed eggs (2 tablespoons ground flaxseed + 6 tablespoons water)
- 1/3 cup chopped hazelnuts
- 1/4 cup dairy-free chocolate chips
- 2 tablespoons maple syrup

Preparation Time:
Total: 3 hours (including rise time)
Instructions:

- *Prepare Flaxseed eggs:*
- In a small bowl, mix 2 tablespoons of ground flaxseed with 6 tablespoons of water. Allow the yeast to sit for a few minutes until it thickens and forms a gel-like consistency.
- *Prepare the Yeast Mixture:*
- In the bread machine pan, combine warm almond milk, cocoa powder, sugar, and yeast. Let the yeast mixture rest for 5-10 minutes until it froths up.
- *Add Wet Ingredients:*
- Pour melted coconut oil into the yeast mixture in the bread machine.
- *Prepare Dry Ingredients:*
- In a bowl, whisk together gluten-free all-purpose flour, xanthan gum, and salt.
- *Combine Ingredients in the Bread Machine:*
- Add the dry ingredients to the bread machine pan over the wet ingredients.
- *Create a Well for Yeast:*
- Make a small well in the center of the dry ingredients and add the yeast.
- *Add Flaxseed eggs:*
- Pour the prepared Flaxseed eggs into the bread machine pan.
- *Set the Bread Machine:*
- Select the gluten-free setting on the bread machine and begin the cycle.
- *Add Hazelnuts and Chocolate Chips*:
- Once the bread machine signals that it's time to add additional ingredients (usually after the initial mixing), add the chopped hazelnuts and dairy-free chocolate chips.
- *Let the Bread Machine Work:*
- Allow the bread machine to complete the cycle. It will mix, knead, and rise the dough.

- *Final Rise and Bake:*
- Once the mixing and rising cycles are complete, leave the dough in the machine for an additional 30 minutes for the final rise and bake.
- *Drizzle with Maple Syrup*
- Once baked, drizzle the warm loaf with maple syrup for added sweetness.

Nutritional Values (per slice):

- Calories: 180
- Protein: 3g
- Fat: 9g
- Carbs: 25g
- Fiber: 3g
- Sugars: 12g

Yield:

Approximately 12 slices

Enjoy:

- Once the baking is complete, carefully remove the gluten-free chocolate hazelnut swirl bread from the machine, and let it cool on a wire rack before slicing.

Ingredients:

- 2 cups gluten-free all-purpose flour
- 1 1/2 teaspoons xanthan gum
- 1/2 cup sugar
- 1 teaspoon ground cinnamon
- 1/2 teaspoon ground nutmeg
- 1 teaspoon salt
- Use 1 packet (2 1/4 teaspoons) of active dry yeast.
- 1 cup unsweetened applesauce
- 1/4 cup melted coconut oil
- 2 Flaxseed eggs (2 tablespoons ground flaxseed + 6 tablespoons water)
- 1 cup diced apples (peeled and cored)

Preparation Time:

Total: 2 hours 30 minutes (including rise time)

Instructions:

- *Prepare Flaxseed eggs:*
- In a small bowl, mix 2 tablespoons of ground flaxseed with 6 tablespoons of water. Allow the yeast to sit for a few minutes until it thickens and forms a gel-like consistency.
- *Prepare the Yeast Mixture:*
- In the bread machine pan, combine applesauce, sugar, ground cinnamon, ground nutmeg, and yeast. Let the yeast mixture rest for 5-10 minutes until it froths up.
- *Add Wet Ingredients:*
- Pour melted coconut oil into the yeast mixture in the bread machine.
- *Prepare Dry Ingredients:*
- In a bowl, whisk together gluten-free all-purpose flour, xanthan gum, and salt.
- *Combine Ingredients in the Bread Machine:*
- Add the dry ingredients to the bread machine pan over the wet ingredients.
- *Create a Well for Yeast:*
- Make a small well in the center of the dry ingredients and add the yeast.
- *Add Flaxseed eggs:*
- Pour the prepared Flaxseed eggs into the bread machine pan.
- *Set the Bread Machine:*
- Select the gluten-free setting on the bread machine and begin the cycle.
- *Add Diced Apples:*
- Once the bread machine signals that it's time to add additional ingredients (usually after the initial mixing), add the diced apples.

- ***Let the Bread Machine Work:***
- Allow the bread machine to complete the cycle. It will mix, knead, and rise the dough.
- ***Final Rise and Bake:***
- Once the mixing and rising cycles are complete, leave the dough in the machine for an additional 30 minutes for the final rise and bake.

Nutritional Values (per slice):

- Calories: 140
- Protein: 2g
- Fat: 6g
- Carbs: 20g
- Fiber: 2g
- Sugars: 8g

Yield:

Approximately 12 slices

Enjoy:

- Once the baking is complete, carefully remove the gluten-free apple cinnamon bread from the machine, and let it cool on a wire rack before slicing.

11. Mediterranean Olive and Herb Bread

Ingredients:

- 1 1/2 cups gluten-free all-purpose flour
- 1 cup almond flour
- 1 1/2 teaspoons xanthan gum
- 1 tablespoon dried oregano
- 1 tablespoon dried thyme
- 1 teaspoon salt
- Use 1 packet (2 1/4 teaspoons) of active dry yeast.
- 1 1/4 cups warm water
- 1/4 cup extra virgin olive oil
- 2 Flaxseed eggs (2 tablespoons ground flaxseed + 6 tablespoons water)
- 1/2 cup sliced Kalamata olives
- 1/4 cup chopped fresh parsley

Preparation Time:

Total: 3 hours (including rise time)

Instructions:

- *Prepare Flaxseed eggs:*
- In a small bowl, mix 2 tablespoons of ground flaxseed with 6 tablespoons of water. Allow the yeast to sit for a few minutes until it thickens and forms a gel-like consistency.
- *Prepare the Yeast Mixture:*
- In the bread machine pan, combine warm water, dried oregano, dried thyme, and yeast. Let the yeast mixture rest for 5-10 minutes until it froths up.
- *Add Wet Ingredients:*
- Pour extra virgin olive oil into the yeast mixture in the bread machine.
- *Prepare Dry Ingredients:*
- In a bowl, whisk together gluten-free all-purpose flour, almond flour, xanthan gum, and salt.
- *Combine Ingredients in the Bread Machine:*
- Add the dry ingredients to the bread machine pan over the wet ingredients.
- *Create a Well for Yeast:*
- Make a small well in the center of the dry ingredients and add the yeast.
- *Add Flaxseed eggs:*
- Pour the prepared Flaxseed eggs into the bread machine pan.
- *Set the Bread Machine:*
- Select the gluten-free setting on the bread machine and begin the cycle.
- **Add Olives and Fresh Parsley:**

- Once the bread machine signals that it's time to add additional ingredients (usually after the initial mixing), add the sliced Kalamata olives and chopped fresh parsley.
- ***Let the Bread Machine Work:***
- Allow the bread machine to complete the cycle. It will mix, knead, and rise the dough.
- ***Final Rise and Bake:***
- Once the mixing and rising cycles are complete, leave the dough in the machine for an additional 30 minutes for the final rise and bake.

Nutritional Values (per slice):

- Calories: 160
- Protein: 4g
- Fat: 8g
- Carbs: 18g
- Fiber: 3g
- Sugars: 1g

Yield:

Approximately 12 slices

Enjoy:

- Once the baking is complete, carefully remove the gluten-free Mediterranean olive and herb bread from the machine, and let it cool on a wire rack before slicing.

12. Sun-Dried Tomato and Basil Bread

Ingredients:
- 2 cups gluten-free all-purpose flour
- 1 1/2 teaspoons xanthan gum
- 1/2 cup sun-dried tomatoes (soaked in warm water and chopped)
- 2 tablespoons chopped fresh basil
- 1 teaspoon garlic powder
- 1 teaspoon onion powder
- 1 teaspoon salt
- Use 1 packet (2 1/4 teaspoons) of active dry yeast.
- 1 1/4 cups warm water
- 1/4 cup olive oil
- 2 Flaxseed eggs (2 tablespoons ground flaxseed + 6 tablespoons water)

Preparation Time:
Total: 3 hours (including rise time)

Instructions:

- ***Prepare Flaxseed eggs:***
- In a small bowl, mix 2 tablespoons of ground flaxseed with 6 tablespoons of water. Allow the yeast to sit for a few minutes until it thickens and forms a gel-like consistency.
- ***Prepare the Yeast Mixture:***
- In the bread machine pan, combine warm water, chopped sun-dried tomatoes, chopped fresh basil, garlic powder, onion powder, and yeast. Let the yeast mixture rest for 5-10 minutes until it froths up.
- ***Add Wet Ingredients:***
- Pour olive oil into the yeast mixture in the bread machine.
- ***Prepare Dry Ingredients:***
- In a bowl, whisk together gluten-free all-purpose flour, xanthan gum, and salt.
- ***Combine Ingredients in the Bread Machine:***
- Add the dry ingredients to the bread machine pan over the wet ingredients.
- ***Create a Well for Yeast:***
- Make a small well in the center of the dry ingredients and add the yeast.
- ***Add Flaxseed eggs:***
- Pour the prepared Flaxseed eggs into the bread machine pan.
- ***Set the Bread Machine:***
- Select the gluten-free setting on the bread machine and begin the cycle.
- ***Let the Bread Machine Work:***
- Allow the bread machine to complete the cycle. It will mix, knead, and rise the dough.
- ***Final Rise and Bake:***

- Once the mixing and rising cycles are complete, leave the dough in the machine for an additional 30 minutes for the final rise and bake.

Nutritional Values (per slice):

- Calories: 150
- Protein: 3g
- Fat: 7g
- Carbs: 20g
- Fiber: 2g
- Sugars: 2g

Yield:

Approximately 12 slices

Enjoy:

- Once the baking is complete, carefully remove the gluten-free sun-dried tomato and basil bread from the machine, and let it cool on a wire rack before slicing.

13. Cranberry Orange Almond Bread

Ingredients:

- 1 1/2 cups gluten-free all-purpose flour
- 1 cup almond flour
- 1 1/2 teaspoons xanthan gum
- 1/2 cup dried cranberries
- Zest of 1 orange
- 1 teaspoon vanilla extract
- 1 teaspoon salt
- Use 1 packet (2 1/4 teaspoons) of active dry yeast.
- 1 1/4 cups warm almond milk
- 1/4 cup melted coconut oil
- 2 flaxseed eggs (2 tablespoons ground flaxseed + 6 tablespoons water)
- 1/4 cup sliced almonds

Preparation Time:
Total: 3 hours (including rise time)
Instructions:
- *Prepare Flaxseed Eggs:*
- In a small bowl, mix 2 tablespoons of ground flaxseed with 6 tablespoons of water. Allow the yeast to sit for a few minutes until it thickens and forms a gel-like consistency.
- *Prepare the Yeast Mixture:*
- In the bread machine pan, combine warm almond milk, dried cranberries, orange zest, vanilla extract, and yeast. Let the yeast mixture rest for 5-10 minutes until it froths up.
- *Add Wet Ingredients:*
- Pour melted coconut oil into the yeast mixture in the bread machine.
- *Prepare Dry Ingredients:*
- In a bowl, whisk together gluten-free all-purpose flour, almond flour, xanthan gum, and salt.
- *Combine Ingredients in the Bread Machine:*
- Add the dry ingredients to the bread machine pan over the wet ingredients.
- *Create a Well for Yeast:*
- Make a small well in the center of the dry ingredients and add the yeast.
- *Add Flaxseed Eggs:*
- Pour the prepared flaxseed eggs into the bread machine pan.
- *Set the Bread Machine:*
- Select the gluten-free setting on the bread machine and begin the cycle.
- *Add Sliced Almonds:*

- Once the bread machine signals that it's time to add additional ingredients (usually after the initial mixing), add the sliced almonds.
- *Let the Bread Machine Work*:
- Allow the bread machine to complete the cycle. It will mix, knead, and rise the dough.
- *Final Rise and Bake:*
- Once the mixing and rising cycles are complete, leave the dough in the machine for an additional 30 minutes for the final rise and bake.

Nutritional Values (per slice):

- Calories: 180
- Protein: 4g
- Fat: 10g
- Carbs: 20g
- Fiber: 3g
- Sugars: 6g

Yield:

Approximately 12 slices

Enjoy:

- Once the baking is complete, carefully remove the gluten-free cranberry orange almond bread from the machine, and let it cool on a wire rack before slicing.

14.Spinach and Feta Savory Bread

Ingredients:
- 2 cups gluten-free all-purpose flour
- 1 1/2 teaspoons xanthan gum
- 1 cup fresh spinach, finely chopped
- 1/2 cup feta cheese, crumbled
- 1/4 cup sun-dried tomatoes, chopped
- 1 teaspoon dried oregano
- 1/2 teaspoon garlic powder
- 1/2 teaspoon salt
- Use 1 packet (2 1/4 teaspoons) of active dry yeast.
- 1 1/4 cups warm almond milk
- 1/4 cup olive oil
- 2 flaxseed eggs (2 tablespoons ground flaxseed + 6 tablespoons water)

Preparation Time:
Total: 3 hours (including rise time)

Instructions:
- ***Prepare Flaxseed Eggs:***

- In a small bowl, mix 2 tablespoons of ground flaxseed with 6 tablespoons of water. Allow the yeast to sit for a few minutes until it thickens and forms a gel-like consistency.
- **_Prepare the Yeast Mixture:_**
- In the bread machine pan, combine warm almond milk, chopped fresh spinach, crumbled feta cheese, sun-dried tomatoes, dried oregano, garlic powder, and yeast. Let the yeast mixture rest for 5-10 minutes until it froths up.
- **_Add Wet Ingredients:_**
- Pour olive oil into the yeast mixture in the bread machine.
- **_Prepare Dry Ingredients:_**
- In a bowl, whisk together gluten-free all-purpose flour, xanthan gum, and salt.
- **_Combine Ingredients in the Bread Machine:_**
- Add the dry ingredients to the bread machine pan over the wet ingredients.
- **_Create a Well for Yeast:_**
- Make a small well in the center of the dry ingredients and add the yeast.
- **_Add Flaxseed Eggs:_**
- Pour the prepared flaxseed eggs into the bread machine pan.
- **_Set the Bread Machine:_**
- Select the gluten-free setting on the bread machine and begin the cycle.
- **_Let the Bread Machine Work_:**
- Allow the bread machine to complete the cycle. It will mix, knead, and rise the dough.
- **_Final Rise and Bake:_**

- Once the mixing and rising cycles are complete, leave the dough in the machine for an additional 30 minutes for the final rise and bake.

Nutritional Values (per slice):

- Calories: 160
- Protein: 4g
- Fat: 7g
- Carbs: 21g
- Fiber: 3g
- Sugars: 1g

Yield:

Approximately 12 slices

Enjoy:

- Once the baking is complete, carefully remove the gluten-free spinach and feta savory bread from the machine, and let it cool on a wire rack before slicing.

15. Chocolate Chip Zucchini Bread

Ingredients:

- 2 cups gluten-free all-purpose flour
- 1 1/2 teaspoons xanthan gum
- 1 cup shredded zucchini (excess moisture squeezed out)
- 1/2 cup dairy-free chocolate chips
- 1/4 cup maple syrup
- 1/4 cup melted coconut oil
- 1 teaspoon vanilla extract
- 1/2 teaspoon cinnamon
- 1/2 teaspoon baking powder
- 1/4 teaspoon baking soda
- 1/4 teaspoon salt
- Use 1 packet (2 1/4 teaspoons) of active dry yeast.
- 1 1/4 cups warm almond milk
- 2 flaxseed eggs (2 tablespoons ground flaxseed + 6 tablespoons water)

Preparation Time:

Total: 3 hours (including rise time)

Instructions:

- ***Prepare Flaxseed Eggs:***

- In a small bowl, mix 2 tablespoons of ground flaxseed with 6 tablespoons of water. Allow the yeast to sit for a few minutes until it thickens and forms a gel-like consistency.
- ***Prepare the Yeast Mixture:***
- In the bread machine pan, combine warm almond milk, shredded zucchini, dairy-free chocolate chips, maple syrup, melted coconut oil, vanilla extract, cinnamon, baking powder, baking soda, and yeast. Let the yeast mixture rest for 5-10 minutes until it froths up.
- ***Add Wet Ingredients:***
- Pour the prepared flaxseed eggs into the yeast mixture in the bread machine.
- ***Prepare Dry Ingredients:***
- In a bowl, whisk together gluten-free all-purpose flour, xanthan gum, and salt.
- ***Combine Ingredients in the Bread Machine:***
- Add the dry ingredients to the bread machine pan over the wet ingredients.
- ***Create a Well for Yeast:***
- Make a small well in the center of the dry ingredients and add the yeast.
- ***Add Flaxseed Eggs:***
- Pour the prepared flaxseed eggs into the bread machine pan.
- ***Set the Bread Machine:***
- Select the gluten-free setting on the bread machine and begin the cycle.
- ***Let the Bread Machine Work***:
- Allow the bread machine to complete the cycle. It will mix, knead, and rise the dough.
- ***Final Rise and Bake:***

- Once the mixing and rising cycles are complete, leave the dough in the machine for an additional 30 minutes for the final rise and bake.

Nutritional Values (per slice):

- Calories: 190
- Protein: 3g
- Fat: 8g
- Carbs: 26g
- Fiber: 3g
- Sugars: 10g

Yield:

Approximately 12 slices

Enjoy:

- Once the baking is complete, carefully remove the gluten-free chocolate chip zucchini bread from the machine, and let it cool on a wire rack before slicing.

16.Herb and Garlic Focaccia

Ingredients:

- 2 cups gluten-free all-purpose flour
- 1 1/2 teaspoons xanthan gum
- 2 tablespoons fresh rosemary, chopped
- 2 tablespoons fresh thyme, chopped
- 3 cloves garlic, minced
- 1/4 cup olive oil
- 1 teaspoon honey
- 1/2 teaspoon salt
- Use 1 packet (2 1/4 teaspoons) of active dry yeast.
- 1 1/4 cups warm almond milk
- 2 flaxseed eggs (2 tablespoons ground flaxseed + 6 tablespoons water)

Preparation Time:

Total: 3 hours (including rise time)

Instructions:

- ***Prepare Flaxseed Eggs:***

- In a small bowl, mix 2 tablespoons of ground flaxseed with 6 tablespoons of water. Allow the yeast to sit for a few minutes until it thickens and forms a gel-like consistency.
- ***Prepare the Yeast Mixture***
- In the bread machine pan, combine warm almond milk, chopped fresh rosemary, chopped fresh thyme, minced garlic, olive oil, honey, and yeast. Let the yeast mixture rest for 5-10 minutes until it froths up.
- ***Add Wet Ingredients:***
- Pour the prepared flaxseed eggs into the yeast mixture in the bread machine.
- ***Prepare Dry Ingredients:***
- In a bowl, whisk together gluten-free all-purpose flour, xanthan gum, and salt.
- ***Combine Ingredients in the Bread Machine:***
- Add the dry ingredients to the bread machine pan over the wet ingredients.
- ***Create a Well for Yeast:***
- Make a small well in the center of the dry ingredients and add the yeast.
- ***Add Flaxseed Eggs:***
- Pour the prepared flaxseed eggs into the bread machine pan.
- ***Set the Bread Machine:***
- Select the gluten-free setting on the bread machine and begin the cycle.
- ***Let the Bread Machine Work***:
- Allow the bread machine to complete the cycle. It will mix, knead, and rise the dough.
- ***Final Rise and Bake:***

- Once the mixing and rising cycles are complete, leave the dough in the machine for an additional 30 minutes for the final rise and bake.

Nutritional Values (per slice):

- Calories: 160
- Protein: 3g
- Fat: 7g
- Carbs: 22g
- Fiber: 2g
- Sugars: 1g

Yield:

Approximately 12 slices

Enjoy:

- Once the baking is complete, carefully remove the gluten-free herb and garlic focaccia from the machine, and let it cool on a wire rack before slicing.

17. Spinach and Artichoke Bread

Ingredients:

- 2 cups gluten-free all-purpose flour
- 1 1/2 teaspoons xanthan gum
- 1/2 cup frozen spinach, thawed and squeezed
- 1/4 cup artichoke hearts, chopped
- 1/4 cup nutritional yeast
- 1/4 cup olive oil
- 1/2 teaspoon garlic powder
- 1/4 teaspoon onion powder
- 1/4 teaspoon salt
- Use 1 packet (2 1/4 teaspoons) of active dry yeast.
- 1 1/4 cups warm almond milk
- 2 flaxseed eggs (2 tablespoons ground flaxseed + 6 tablespoons water)

Instructions:

- *Prepare Flaxseed Eggs:*

- Mix 2 tablespoons of ground flaxseed with 6 tablespoons of water in a small bowl. Allow the mixture to sit until it thickens to the desired consistency.
- *Yeast Mixture:*
- In the bread machine pan, combine warm almond milk, thawed and squeezed spinach, chopped artichoke hearts, nutritional yeast, olive oil, garlic powder, onion powder, and salt. Let the yeast mixture rest for 5-10 minutes until it froths up.
- *Wet Ingredients:*
- Pour the prepared flaxseed eggs into the yeast mixture in the bread machine.
- *Dry Ingredients:*
- Whisk together gluten-free all-purpose flour, xanthan gum, and salt in a separate bowl.
- *Combine Ingredients:*
- Add the dry ingredients to the bread machine pan over the wet ingredients.
- *Create Well for Yeast:*
- Make a small well in the center of the dry ingredients and add the yeast.
- *Add Flaxseed Eggs:*
- Pour the prepared flaxseed eggs into the bread machine pan.
- *Bread Machine Settings:*
- Select the gluten-free setting on the bread machine and begin the cycle.
- *Let the Bread Machine Work:*
- Allow the machine to complete the cycle, including mixing, kneading, and rising.
- *Final Rise and Bake:*
- After the mixing and rising cycles, leave the dough for an additional 30 minutes for the final rise and bake.

Nutritional Values (per slice):

- Calories: 160
- Protein: 3g
- Fat: 8g
- Carbs: 21g
- Fiber: 2g
- Sugars: 1g

Yield:

Approximately 12 slices

Enjoy:

- Once baked, carefully remove the gluten-free spinach and artichoke bread from the machine and let it cool on a wire rack before slicing.

Ingredients:

- 2 cups gluten-free all-purpose flour
- 1 1/2 teaspoons xanthan gum
- 2 tablespoons fresh rosemary, chopped
- 2 cloves garlic, minced
- 1/4 cup olive oil
- 1 teaspoon salt
- Use 1 packet (2 1/4 teaspoons) of active dry yeast.
- 1 1/4 cups warm almond milk
- 2 flaxseed eggs (2 tablespoons ground flaxseed + 6 tablespoons water)

Instructions:

- *Prepare Flaxseed Eggs:*

- Mix 2 tablespoons of ground flaxseed with 6 tablespoons of water in a small bowl. Allow the mixture to sit until it thickens to the desired consistency.
- *Yeast Mixture:*
- In the bread machine pan, combine warm almond milk, chopped fresh rosemary, minced garlic, olive oil, and salt. Let the yeast mixture rest for 5-10 minutes until it froths up.
- *Wet Ingredients:*
- Pour the prepared flaxseed eggs into the yeast mixture in the bread machine.
- *Dry Ingredients:*
- Whisk together gluten-free all-purpose flour, xanthan gum, and salt in a separate bowl.
- *Combine Ingredients:*
- Add the dry ingredients to the bread machine pan over the wet ingredients.
- *Create Well for Yeast:*
- Make a small well in the center of the dry ingredients and add the yeast.
- *Add Flaxseed Eggs:*
- Pour the prepared flaxseed eggs into the bread machine pan.
- *Bread Machine Settings:*
- Select the gluten-free setting on the bread machine and begin the cycle.
- *Let the Bread Machine Work:*
- Allow the machine to complete the cycle, including mixing, kneading, and rising.
- *Final Rise and Bake:*
- After the mixing and rising cycles, leave the dough for an additional 30 minutes for the final rise and bake.

Nutritional Values (per slice):

- Calories: 160
- Protein: 3g
- Fat: 8g
- Carbs: 20g
- Fiber: 2g
- Sugars: 0g

Yield:

Approximately 12 slices

Enjoy:

- Once baked, carefully remove the gluten-free rosemary garlic focaccia from the machine and let it cool on a wire rack before slicing.

19. Herbed Tomato Bread

Ingredients:
- 2 cups gluten-free all-purpose flour
- 1 1/2 teaspoons xanthan gum
- 1/2 cup sun-dried tomatoes, chopped
- 2 tablespoons fresh basil, chopped
- 1 tablespoon fresh oregano, chopped
- 1/4 cup olive oil
- 1/4 teaspoon salt
- Use 1 packet (2 1/4 teaspoons) of active dry yeast.
- 1 1/4 cups warm almond milk
- 2 flaxseed eggs (2 tablespoons ground flaxseed + 6 tablespoons water)

Instructions:
- ***Prepare Flaxseed Eggs:***

- Mix 2 tablespoons of ground flaxseed with 6 tablespoons of water in a small bowl. Allow the mixture to sit until it thickens to the desired consistency.
- *Yeast Mixture:*
- In the bread machine pan, combine warm almond milk, chopped sun-dried tomatoes, fresh basil, fresh oregano, olive oil, and salt. Let the yeast mixture rest for 5-10 minutes until it froths up.
- *Wet Ingredients:*
- Pour the prepared flaxseed eggs into the yeast mixture in the bread machine.
- *Dry Ingredients:*
- Whisk together gluten-free all-purpose flour, xanthan gum, and salt in a separate bowl.
- *Combine Ingredients:*
- Add the dry ingredients to the bread machine pan over the wet ingredients.
- *Create Well for Yeast:*
- Make a small well in the center of the dry ingredients and add the yeast.
- *Add Flaxseed Eggs:*
- Pour the prepared flaxseed eggs into the bread machine pan.
- *Bread Machine Settings:*
- Select the gluten-free setting on the bread machine and begin the cycle.
- *Let the Bread Machine Work*:
- Allow the machine to complete the cycle, including mixing, kneading, and rising.
- *Final Rise and Bake:*
- After the mixing and rising cycles, leave the dough for an additional 30 minutes for the final rise and bake.

Nutritional Values (per slice):

- Calories: 170
- Protein: 3g
- Fat: 8g
- Carbs: 21g
- Fiber: 2g
- Sugars: 1g

Yield:

Approximately 12 slices

Enjoy:

- Once baked, carefully remove the gluten-free herbed tomato bread from the machine and let it cool on a wire rack before slicing.

Chia Seed Multigrain Bread

Ingredients:

- 1 1/2 cups gluten-free all-purpose flour
- 1 cup gluten-free oat flour
- 1/2 cup quinoa flour
- 1/4 cup chia seeds
- 1/4 cup sunflower seeds
- 1/4 cup flaxseeds
- 1/4 cup melted coconut oil
- 1/4 cup honey
- 1 teaspoon salt
- Use 1 packet (2 1/4 teaspoons) of active dry yeast.
- 1 1/4 cups warm almond milk
- 2 flaxseed eggs (2 tablespoons ground flaxseed + 6 tablespoons water)

Instructions:

- *Prepare Flaxseed Eggs:*

- Mix 2 tablespoons of ground flaxseed with 6 tablespoons of water in a small bowl. Allow the mixture to sit until it thickens to the desired consistency.
- *Yeast Mixture:*
- In the bread machine pan, combine warm almond milk, chia seeds, sunflower seeds, flaxseeds, melted coconut oil, honey, and salt. Let the yeast mixture rest for 5-10 minutes until it froths up.
- *Wet Ingredients:*
- Pour the prepared flaxseed eggs into the yeast mixture in the bread machine.
- *Dry Ingredients:*
- Whisk together gluten-free all-purpose flour, oat flour, quinoa flour, and salt in a separate bowl.
- *Combine Ingredients:*
- Add the dry ingredients to the bread machine pan over the wet ingredients.
- *Create Well for Yeast:*
- Make a small well in the center of the dry ingredients and add the yeast.
- *Add Flaxseed Eggs:*
- Pour the prepared flaxseed eggs into the bread machine pan.
- *Bread Machine Settings:*
- Select the gluten-free setting on the bread machine and begin the cycle
- *Let the Bread Machine Work:*
- Allow the machine to complete the cycle, including mixing, kneading, and rising.
- *Final Rise and Bake:*
- After the mixing and rising cycles, leave the dough for an additional 30 minutes for the final rise and bake.

Nutritional Values (per slice):

- Calories: 160
- Protein: 4g
- Fat: 7g
- Carbs: 22g
- Fiber: 3g
- Sugars: 5g

<u>Yield:</u>

Approximately 12 slices

<u>Enjoy:</u>

- Once baked, carefully remove the gluten-free Chia Seed Multigrain bread from the machine and let it cool on a wire rack before slicing.

21. Gluten-Free Quinoa Bread

Ingredients:

- 1 1/2 cups quinoa flour
- 1 1/2 cups gluten-free oat flour
- 1/2 cup tapioca flour
- 1/4 cup ground flaxseed
- 2 teaspoons active dry yeast
- 1 teaspoon salt
- 1 tablespoon honey
- 3 large Flaxseed eggs
- 1 cup unsweetened almond milk
- 1/4 cup olive oil

Instructions:

- Place all dry ingredients into the bread machine pan.
- In a separate bowl, whisk together Flaxseed eggs, almond milk, and honey.
- Pour the wet ingredients into the bread machine pan over the dry ingredients.
- Add olive oil to the mixture.
- Create a hollow in the middle of the dry ingredients and incorporate the yeast.
- Place the bread machine pan into the machine and select the gluten-free setting.
- Set the machine to a 2-pound loaf size and start the cycle.
- Afterward, ensure the bread is cooled down before cutting into slices.

Nutritional Information (per slice, calculated for 16 slices):

- Calories: 120
- Protein: 4g
- Fat: 5g
- Carbohydrates: 15g
- Fiber: 2g
- Sugars: 1g

Yield:

One 2-pound loaf (approximately 16 slices)

Preparation Time:

10 minutes (excluding bread machine time)

Ingredients:

- 1 1/2 cups coconut flour
- 1/2 cup almond flour
- 1/4 cup raisins
- 2 teaspoons active dry yeast
- 1 teaspoon cinnamon
- 1 tablespoon maple syrup
- 4 large Flaxseed eggs
- 1 cup warm almond milk
- 1/4 cup coconut oil

Instructions:

- Place all dry ingredients into the bread machine pan.
- In a separate bowl, whisk together Flaxseed eggs, warm almond milk, maple syrup, and melted coconut oil.

- Pour the wet ingredients into the bread machine pan over the dry ingredients.
- Create a hollow in the middle of the dry ingredients and incorporate the yeast.
- Set the machine to a gluten-free setting with a 2-pound loaf size.
- Start the cycle. Prior to slicing, allow the bread to cool.

Nutritional Information (per slice, calculated for 16 slices):

- Calories: 140
- Protein: 5g
- Fat: 7g
- Carbohydrates: 16g
- Fiber: 3g
- Sugars: 4g

Yield:

One 2-pound loaf (approximately 16 slices)

Ingredients:

- 2 cups gluten-free all-purpose flour
- 1 cup brown rice flour
- 1/2 cup tapioca flour
- 1/4 cup flaxseed meal
- 2 teaspoons active dry yeast
- 1 1/2 teaspoons xanthan gum
- 1 teaspoon salt
- 2 tablespoons honey
- 3 large Flaxseed eggs
- 1 1/4 cups warm water
- 1/4 cup olive oil

Instructions:

- ***Prepare Bread Machine:***

- Make sure your bread machine is clean and dry.
- Insert the mixing paddle into the bread pan.
- ***Combine Dry Ingredients:***
- In a large mixing bowl, combine gluten-free all-purpose flour, brown rice flour, tapioca flour, flaxseed meal, active dry yeast, xanthan gum, and salt.
- ***Mix Wet Ingredients:***
- In a separate bowl, whisk together honey, Flaxseed eggs, warm water, and olive oil.
- ***Combine Mixtures:***
- Add the wet ingredients to the dry ingredients. Thoroughly combine the ingredients until a smooth batter is achieved. It will be thicker than traditional bread dough.
- ***Add to Bread Machine:***
- Transfer the batter to the pan of the bread machine.
- ***Set Bread Machine:***
- Close the lid of the bread machine and set it to the gluten-free setting.
- Choose the 2-pound loaf size if your machine allows for different sizes.
- ***Start the Machine:***
- Initiate the bread machine cycle by pressing the start button.
- ***Wait and Cool:***
- Allow the machine to run its course. Gluten-free cycles typically take longer than regular cycles.

- Once done, carefully remove the bread pan and let the bread cool in the pan for about 10 minutes.
- ***Remove and Cool Further:***
- Gently take out the bread from the pan and position it on a wire rack for complete cooling.
- ***Slice and Enjoy:***
- Once the bread has completely cooled, proceed to slice and savor its delightful taste!

Nutritional Information (per slice, calculated for 16 slices):

- Calories: 120
- Protein: 3g
- Fat: 5g
- Carbohydrates: 18g
- Fiber: 2g
- Sugars: 2g

Yield:

One 2-pound loaf (approximately 16 slices)

Buckwheat & Sunflower Seed Bread

Ingredients:

- 1 1/2 cups buckwheat flour
- 1/2 cup brown rice flour
- 1/4 cup sunflower seeds
- 2 teaspoons active dry yeast
- 1 teaspoon salt
- 1 tablespoon honey
- 3 large Flaxseed eggs
- 1 1/4 cups warm water
- 1/4 cup olive oil

Instructions:

- *Combine Dry Ingredients:*
- In a large mixing bowl, whisk together buckwheat flour, brown rice flour, sunflower seeds, yeast, and salt.
- *Prepare Wet Ingredients:*
- In a separate bowl, combine honey, Flaxseed eggs, warm water, and olive oil. Whisk until well blended.
- *Mix Wet and Dry Ingredients:*
- Combine the wet ingredients by pouring them into the bowl containing the dry ingredients. Stir until a smooth batter forms.
- *Transfer to Bread Machine:*
- Pour the batter into the bread machine pan, ensuring an even distribution.
- *Set the Bread Machine:*
- Set the bread machine to the gluten-free setting and choose the 2-pound loaf size.
- *Initiate the Machine:*
- Initiate the bread machine cycle by pressing the start button.
- *Cool and Slice:*
- Once the cycle is complete, wait for 10 minutes before carefully removing the bread from the pan.
- Afterwards, transfer the bread to a wire rack and ensure it cools down completely before proceeding with slicing.

Nutritional Information (per slice, calculated for 16 slices):

- Calories: 120
- Protein: 3.5g
- Fat: 4.5g
- Carbs: 15g
- Fiber: 2g
- Sugars: 1.5g

Ingredients:

- 1 1/2 cups brown rice flour
- 1/2 cup sorghum flour
- 1/4 cup chia seeds
- 2 teaspoons active dry yeast
- 1 teaspoon salt
- 1 tablespoon maple syrup
- 4 large Flaxseed eggs
- 1 cup warm water
- 1/4 cup olive oil

Instructions:

- ***Combine Dry Ingredients:***

- In a large mixing bowl, whisk together brown rice flour, sorghum flour, chia seeds, yeast, and salt.

- *Prepare Wet Ingredients:*
- In a separate bowl, combine maple syrup, Flaxseed eggs, warm water, and olive oil. Whisk until well blended.
- *Mix Wet and Dry Ingredients:*
- Combine the wet ingredients by pouring them into the bowl containing the dry ingredients. Stir until a smooth batter forms.
- *Transfer to Bread Machine:*
- Pour the batter into the bread machine pan, ensuring an even distribution.
- *Set the Bread Machine:*
- Set the bread machine to the gluten-free setting and choose the 2-pound loaf size.
- *Initiate the Machine:*
- Initiate the bread machine cycle by pressing the start button.
- *Cool and Slice:*
- Once the cycle is complete, wait for 10 minutes before carefully removing the bread from the pan.
- Afterwards, transfer the bread to a wire rack and ensure it cools down completely before proceeding with slicing.

Nutritional Information (per slice, calculated for 16 slices):

- Calories: 130
- Protein: 4.5g
- Fat: 6g

- Carbs: 16g
- Fiber: 2.5g
- Sugars: 2g

Sweet And Savory Bread Recipes

26.   Hazelnut & Cranberry Bread

Ingredients:

- 1 1/2 cups hazelnut flour
- 1/2 cup arrowroot flour
- 1/4 cup dried cranberries
- 2 teaspoons active dry yeast
- 1 teaspoon salt
- 1 tablespoon honey
- 3 large Flaxseed eggs
- 1 1/4 cups warm water
- 1/4 cup olive oil

Instructions:

- *Combine Dry Ingredients:*
- In a large mixing bowl, whisk together hazelnut flour, arrowroot flour, dried cranberries, yeast, and salt.
- *Prepare Wet Ingredients:*
- In a separate bowl, combine honey, Flaxseed eggs, warm water, and olive oil. Whisk until well blended.
- *Mix Wet and Dry Ingredients:*
- Combine the wet ingredients by pouring them into the bowl containing the dry ingredients Stir until a smooth batter forms.
- *Transfer to Bread Machine:*

- Pour the batter into the bread machine pan, making sure it's evenly distributed.
- ***Set the Bread Machine:***
- Set the bread machine to the gluten-free setting and choose the 2-pound loaf size.
- ***Initiate the Machine:***
- Initiate the bread machine cycle by pressing the start button.
- ***Cool and Slice:***
- After the cycle completes, wait for 10 minutes before carefully removing the bread from the pan.
- Afterwards, transfer the bread to a wire rack and ensure it cools down completely before proceeding with slicing.

Nutritional Information (per slice, calculated for 16 slices):

- Calories: 130
- Protein: 3.5g
- Fat: 6g
- Carbs: 15g
- Fiber: 2g
- Sugars: 2.5g

Ingredients:

1 1/2 cups amaranth flour

1 cup pecan flour

1/4 cup chopped pecans

2 teaspoons active dry yeast

1 teaspoon salt

1 tablespoon maple syrup

4 large Flaxseed eggs

1 cup warm water

1/4 cup olive oil

Instructions:

- ***Combine Dry Ingredients:***
- In a large mixing bowl, whisk together amaranth flour, pecan flour, chopped pecans, yeast, and salt.

- ***Prepare Wet Ingredients:***
- In a separate bowl, combine maple syrup, Flaxseed eggs, warm water, and olive oil. Whisk until well blended.

- ***Mix Wet and Dry Ingredients:***
- Combine the wet ingredients by pouring them into the bowl containing the dry ingredients Stir until a smooth batter forms.

- ***Transfer to Bread Machine:***

- Pour the batter into the bread machine pan, ensuring an even distribution.
- ***Set the Bread Machine:***
- Set the bread machine to the gluten-free setting and choose the 2-pound loaf size.
- ***Initiate the Machine:***
- Initiate the bread machine cycle by pressing the start button.
- ***Cool and Slice:***
- Once the cycle is complete, wait for 10 minutes before carefully removing the bread from the pan.
- Afterwards, transfer the bread to a wire rack and ensure it cools down completely before proceeding with slicing.

Nutritional Information (per slice, calculated for 16 slices):

Calories: 140
Protein: 4.5g
Fat: 7g
Carbs: 14g
Fiber: 2.5g
Sugars: 2g

28.   Sesame Seed & Teff Bread

Ingredients:

- 1 1/2 cups teff flour
- 1/2 cup sesame seed flour
- 1/4 cup sesame seeds
- 2 teaspoons active dry yeast
- 1 teaspoon salt
- 1 tablespoon honey
- 3 large Flaxseed eggs
- 1 1/4 cups warm water
- 1/4 cup olive oil

Instructions:

- *Combine Dry Ingredients*
- In a large mixing bowl, combine teff flour, sesame seed flour, sesame seeds, yeast, and salt.
- *Prepare Wet Ingredients:*
- In a separate bowl, mix honey, Flaxseed eggs, warm water, and olive oil.
- *Mix Wet and Dry Ingredients:*
- Combine the wet ingredients by pouring them into the bowl containing the dry ingredients. Stir until a smooth batter forms.
- *Transfer to Bread Machine:*

- Pour the batter into the pan of the bread machine.
- ***Set the Bread Machine:***
- Set the machine to the gluten-free setting and choose the 2-pound loaf size.
- ***Initiate the Machine:***
- Press the start button to commence the bread machine cycle.
- ***Cool and Slice:***
- After the cycle completes, wait for 10 minutes before carefully removing the bread from the pan.
- Afterwards, transfer the bread to a wire rack and ensure it cools down completely before proceeding with slicing.

Nutritional Information (per slice, calculated for 16 slices):

- Calories: 110
- Protein: 3.5g
- Fat: 5g
- Carbs: 15g
- Fiber: 2g
- Sugars: 2g

Pumpkin Seed & Amaranth Bread

Ingredients:

- 1 1/2 cups amaranth flour
- 1/2 cup pumpkin seed flour
- 1/4 cup pumpkin seeds
- 2 teaspoons active dry yeast
- 1 teaspoon salt
- 1 tablespoon maple syrup
- 4 large Flaxseed eggs
- 1 cup warm water
- 1/4 cup olive oil

Instructions:

- *Combine Dry Ingredients:*
- In a large mixing bowl, combine amaranth flour, pumpkin seed flour, pumpkin seeds, yeast, and salt.
- *Prepare Wet Ingredients:*
- In a separate bowl, whisk together maple syrup, Flaxseed eggs, warm water, and olive oil.
- *Mix Wet and Dry Ingredients:*
- Combine the wet ingredients by pouring them into the bowl containing the dry ingredients. Stir until a smooth batter forms.
- *Transfer to Bread Machine:*

- Pour the batter into the pan of the bread machine.
- ***Set the Bread Machine:***
- Set the machine to the gluten-free setting and choose the 2-pound loaf size.
- ***Initiate the Machine:***
- Press the start button to commence the bread machine cycle.
- ***Cool and Slice:***
- After the cycle completes, wait for 10 minutes before carefully removing the bread from the pan.
- Afterwards, transfer the bread to a wire rack and ensure it cools down completely before proceeding with slicing.

Nutritional Information (per slice, calculated for 16 slices):

- Calories: 130
- Protein: 4g
- Fat: 6g
- Carbs: 16g
- Fiber: 2.5g
- Sugars: 2g

30. Coconut Flour & Pine Nut Bread

Ingredients:

- 1 1/2 cups coconut flour
- 1/2 cup almond flour
- 1/4 cup pine nuts
- 2 teaspoons active dry yeast
- 1 teaspoon salt
- 1 tablespoon honey
- 4 large Flaxseed eggs
- 1 cup warm almond milk
- 1/4 cup coconut oil

Instructions:

Combine Dry Ingredients:

- In a large mixing bowl, combine coconut flour, almond flour, pine nuts, yeast, and salt.
- *Prepare Wet Ingredients:*
- In a separate bowl, whisk together honey, Flaxseed eggs, warm almond milk, and melted coconut oil.
- *Mix Wet and Dry Ingredients:*
- Combine the wet ingredients by pouring them into the bowl containing the dry ingredients. Stir until a smooth batter forms.
- *Transfer to Bread Machine:*

- Pour the batter into the pan of the bread machine.
- ***Set the Bread Machine:***
- Set the machine to the gluten-free setting and choose the 2-pound loaf size.
- ***Initiate the Machine:***
- Press the start button to commence the bread machine cycle.
- ***Cool and Slice:***
- After the cycle completes, wait for 10 minutes before carefully removing the bread from the pan.
- Afterwards, transfer the bread to a wire rack and ensure it cools down completely before proceeding with slicing.

Nutritional Information (per slice, calculated for 16 slices):

- Calories: 140
- Protein: 5g
- Fat: 7g
- Carbs: 16g
- Fiber: 3g
- Sugars: 2g

31. Cinnamon Raisin & Oat Bread

Ingredients:

- 1 1/2 cups oat flour (certified gluten-free)
- 1/2 cup almond flour
- 1/4 cup raisins
- 2 teaspoons active dry yeast
- 1 teaspoon cinnamon
- 1 tablespoon maple syrup
- 4 large Flaxseed eggs
- 1 cup warm almond milk
- 1/4 cup coconut oil

Instructions:

- ***Combine in the Bread Machine:***
- Place all dry ingredients (oat flour, almond flour, raisins, yeast, and cinnamon) into the bread machine.
- ***Prepare Wet Ingredients:***
- In a separate bowl, whisk together maple syrup, Flaxseed eggs, warm almond milk, and melted coconut oil.
- ***Add Wet Ingredients to the Bread Machine:***
- Combine the wet ingredients by pouring them into the bowl containing the dry ingredients.
- ***Mix in the Bread Machine:***

- Set the bread machine to the gluten-free setting and 2-pound loaf size.
- Press the start button to begin the mixing and kneading process.
- ***Pause and Add Mix-Ins:***
- When the machine signals the addition of mix-ins (usually indicated by a beep), add raisins.
- ***Complete the Cycle:***
- Allow the machine to run through the entire cycle.
- ***Cool and Slice:***
- After the cycle is complete, wait for 10 minutes before carefully removing the bread from the pan.
- Afterwards, transfer the bread to a wire rack and ensure it cools down completely before proceeding with slicing.

Nutritional Information (per slice, calculated for 16 slices):

- Calories: 140
- Protein: 5g
- Fat: 7g
- Carbs: 16g
- Fiber: 3g
- Sugars: 2g

Ingredients:

- 1 1/2 cups flaxseed meal
- 1/2 cup walnut flour
- 1/4 cup chopped walnuts
- 2 teaspoons active dry yeast
- 1 teaspoon salt
- 1 tablespoon honey
- 3 large Flaxseed eggs
- 1 1/4 cups warm water
- 1/4 cup olive oil

Instructions:

- *Combine in the Bread Machine:*
- Place flaxseed meal, walnut flour, chopped walnuts, yeast, and salt into the bread machine.
- *Prepare Wet Ingredients:*
- In a separate bowl, whisk together honey, Flaxseed eggs, warm water, and olive oil.
- *Add Wet Ingredients to the Bread Machine:*
- Pour the wet ingredients into the bread machine over the dry ingredients.
- *Mix in the Bread Machine:*

- Set the bread machine to the gluten-free setting and 2-pound loaf size.
- Press the start button to begin the mixing and kneading process.
- ***Pause and Add Mix-Ins:***
- When the machine signals the addition of mix-ins (usually indicated by a beep), add chopped walnuts.
- ***Complete the Cycle:***
- Allow the machine to run through the entire cycle.
- ***Cool and Slice:***
- After the cycle is complete, wait for 10 minutes before carefully removing the bread from the pan.
- Afterwards, transfer the bread to a wire rack and ensure it cools down completely before proceeding with slicing.

Nutritional Information (per slice, calculated for 16 slices):

- Calories: 130
- Protein: 4.5g
- Fat: 6g
- Carbs: 15g
- Fiber: 2.5g
- Sugars: 2g

Ingredients:

- 1 1/2 cups sorghum flour
- 1 cup millet flour
- 1/4 cup pumpkin seeds
- 2 teaspoons active dry yeast
- 1 teaspoon salt
- 1 tablespoon molasses
- 3 large Flaxseed eggs
- 1 1/2 cups warm water
- 1/4 cup olive oil

Instructions:

- *Combine in the Bread Machine:*
- Place sorghum flour, millet flour, pumpkin seeds, yeast, and salt into the bread machine.
- *Prepare Wet Ingredients:*
- In a separate bowl, whisk together molasses, Flaxseed eggs, warm water, and olive oil.
- *Add Wet Ingredients to the Bread Machine:*
- Pour the wet ingredients into the bread machine over the dry ingredients.
- *Mix in the Bread Machine:*

- Set the bread machine to the gluten-free setting and 2-pound loaf size.
- Press the start button to begin the mixing and kneading process.
- ***Pause and Add Mix-Ins:***
- When the machine signals the addition of mix-ins (usually indicated by a beep), add pumpkin seeds.
- ***Complete the Cycle:***
- Allow the machine to run through the entire cycle.
- ***Cool and Slice:***
- After the cycle is complete, wait for 10 minutes before carefully removing the bread from the pan.
- Afterwards, transfer the bread to a wire rack and ensure it cools down completely before proceeding with slicing.

Nutritional Information (per slice, calculated for 16 slices):

- Calories: 120
- Protein: 3.5g
- Fat: 4.5g
- Carbs: 15g
- Fiber: 2g
- Sugars: 1.5g

Ingredients:

- 1 1/2 cups buckwheat flour
- 1/2 cup oat flour (certified gluten-free)
- 1/4 cup mashed sweet potato
- 2 teaspoons active dry yeast
- 1 teaspoon cinnamon
- 1 tablespoon honey
- 3 large Flaxseed eggs
- 1 1/4 cups warm water
- 1/4 cup olive oil

Instructions:

- *Combine in the Bread Machine:*
- Place buckwheat flour, oat flour, mashed sweet potato, yeast, and cinnamon into the bread machine.
- *Prepare Wet Ingredients:*
- In a separate bowl, whisk together honey, Flaxseed eggs, warm water, and olive oil.
- *Add Wet Ingredients to the Bread Machine:*
- Pour the wet ingredients into the bread machine over the dry ingredients.
- *Mix in the Bread Machine:*

- Set the bread machine to the gluten-free setting and 2-pound loaf size.
- Press the start button to begin the mixing and kneading process.
- ***Pause and Add Mix-Ins:***
- When the machine signals the addition of mix-ins (usually indicated by a beep), add mashed sweet potato.
- ***Complete the Cycle:***
- Allow the machine to run through the entire cycle.
- ***Cool and Slice:***
- After the cycle is complete, wait for 10 minutes before carefully removing the bread from the pan.
- Afterwards, transfer the bread to a wire rack and ensure it cools down completely before proceeding with slicing.

Nutritional Information (per slice, calculated for 16 slices):

- Calories: 130

Protein: 4g

Fat: 6g

Carbs: 15g

Fiber: 2.5g

Sugars: 2g

Ingredients:

- 1 1/2 cups hazelnut flour
- 1/2 cup almond flour
- 1/4 cup chopped dried apricots
- 2 teaspoons active dry yeast
- 1 teaspoon salt
- 1 tablespoon honey
- 3 large Flaxseed eggs
- 1 1/4 cups warm water
- 1/4 cup olive oil

Instructions:

- ***Combine in the Bread Machine:***
- Place hazelnut flour, almond flour, chopped dried apricots, yeast, and salt into the bread machine.
- ***Prepare Wet Ingredients:***
- In a separate bowl, whisk together honey, Flaxseed eggs, warm water, and olive oil.
- ***Add Wet Ingredients to the Bread Machine:***
- Pour the wet ingredients into the bread machine over the dry ingredients.
- ***Mix in the Bread Machine:***

- Set the bread machine to the gluten-free setting and 2-pound loaf size.
- Press the start button to begin the mixing and kneading process.
- ***Pause and Add Mix-Ins:***
- When the machine signals the addition of mix-ins (usually indicated by a beep), add chopped dried apricots.
- ***Complete the Cycle:***
- Allow the machine to run through the entire cycle.
- ***Cool and Slice:***
- After the cycle is complete, wait for 10 minutes before carefully removing the bread from the pan.
- Afterwards, transfer the bread to a wire rack and ensure it cools down completely before proceeding with slicing.

Nutritional Information (per slice, calculated for 16 slices):

- Calories: 140
- Protein: 5g
- Fat: 7g
- Carbs: 16g
- Fiber: 2.5g
- Sugars: 2.5g

Ingredients:

- 1 1/2 cups millet flour
- 1/2 cup almond flour
- 1/4 cup dried cranberries
- 2 teaspoons active dry yeast
- 1 teaspoon cinnamon
- 1 tablespoon maple syrup
- 4 large Flaxseed eggs
- 1 cup warm almond milk
- 1/4 cup coconut oil

Instructions:

- *Combine in the Bread Machine:*
- Place millet flour, almond flour, dried cranberries, yeast, and cinnamon into the bread machine.
- *Prepare Wet Ingredients:*
- In a separate bowl, whisk together maple syrup, Flaxseed eggs, warm almond milk, and melted coconut oil.
- *Add Wet Ingredients to the Bread Machine:*
- Pour the wet ingredients into the bread machine over the dry ingredients.
- *Mix in the Bread Machine:*

- Set the bread machine to the gluten-free setting and 2-pound loaf size.
- Press the start button to begin the mixing and kneading process.
- ***Pause and Add Mix-Ins:***
- When the machine signals the addition of mix-ins (usually indicated by a beep), add dried cranberries.
- ***Complete the Cycle:***
- Allow the machine to run through the entire cycle.
- ***Cool and Slice:***
- After the cycle is complete, wait for 10 minutes before carefully removing the bread from the pan.
- Afterwards, transfer the bread to a wire rack and ensure it cools down completely before proceeding with slicing.

Nutritional Information (per slice, calculated for 16 slices):

- Calories: 130
- Protein: 4.5g
- Fat: 6g
- Carbs: 16g
- Fiber: 2.5g
- Sugars: 2.5g

Quinoa & Pecan Bread

Ingredients:

- 1 1/2 cups quinoa flour
- 1/2 cup pecan flour
- 1/4 cup chopped pecans
- 2 teaspoons active dry yeast
- 1 teaspoon salt
- 1 tablespoon honey
- 3 large Flaxseed eggs
- 1 1/4 cups warm water
- 1/4 cup olive oil

Instructions:

- *Combine in the Bread Machine:*
- Place quinoa flour, pecan flour, chopped pecans, yeast, and salt into the bread machine.
- *Prepare Wet Ingredients:*
- In a separate bowl, whisk together honey, Flaxseed eggs, warm water, and olive oil.
- *Add Wet Ingredients to the Bread Machine:*
- Pour the wet ingredients into the bread machine over the dry ingredients.
- *Mix in the Bread Machine:*

- Set the bread machine to the gluten-free setting and 2-pound loaf size.
- Press the start button to begin the mixing and kneading process.
- ***Pause and Add Mix-Ins:***
- When the machine signals the addition of mix-ins (usually indicated by a beep), add chopped pecans.
- ***Complete the Cycle:***
- Allow the machine to run through the entire cycle.
- ***Cool and Slice:***
- After the cycle is complete, wait for 10 minutes before carefully removing the bread from the pan.
- Afterwards, transfer the bread to a wire rack and ensure it cools down completely before proceeding with slicing.

Nutritional Information (per slice, calculated for 16 slices):

- Calories: 140
- Protein: 5g
- Fat: 7g
- Carbs: 16g
- Fiber: 3g
- Sugars: 2g

38.   Coconut & Chia Seed Bread

Ingredients:

- 1 1/2 cups coconut flour
- 1/2 cup almond flour
- 1/4 cup chia seeds
- 2 teaspoons active dry yeast
- 1 teaspoon salt
- 1 tablespoon maple syrup
- 4 large Flaxseed eggs
- 1 cup warm water
- 1/4 cup olive oil

Instructions:

- *Combine in the Bread Machine:*
- Place coconut flour, almond flour, chia seeds, yeast, and salt into the bread machine.
- *Prepare Wet Ingredients:*
- In a separate bowl, combine maple syrup, Flaxseed eggs, warm water, and olive oil. Whisk until well blended.
- *Add Wet Ingredients to the Bread Machine:*
- Pour the wet ingredients into the bread machine over the dry ingredients.
- *Mix in the Bread Machine:*

- Set the bread machine to the gluten-free setting and 2-pound loaf size.
- Press the start button to begin the mixing and kneading process.
- ***Pause and Add Mix-Ins:***
- When the machine signals the addition of mix-ins (usually indicated by a beep), add chia seeds.
- ***Complete the Cycle:***
- Allow the machine to run through the entire cycle.
- ***Cool and Slice:***
- After the cycle is complete, wait for 10 minutes before carefully removing the bread from the pan.
- Afterwards, transfer the bread to a wire rack and ensure it cools down completely before proceeding with slicing.

Nutritional Information (per slice, calculated for 16 slices):

- Calories: 130
- Protein: 4.5g
- Fat: 6g
- Carbs: 16g
- Fiber: 2.5g
- Sugars: 2g

Ingredients:

- 1 1/2 cups amaranth flour
- 1/2 cup sunflower seed flour
- 1/4 cup sunflower seeds
- 2 teaspoons active dry yeast
- 1 teaspoon salt
- 1 tablespoon honey
- 3 large Flaxseed eggs
- 1 1/4 cups warm water
- 1/4 cup olive oil

Instructions:

- *Combine in the Bread Machine:*
- Place amaranth flour, sunflower seed flour, sunflower seeds, yeast, and salt into the bread machine.
- *Prepare Wet Ingredients:*
- In a separate bowl, whisk together honey, Flaxseed eggs, warm water, and olive oil.
- *Add Wet Ingredients to the Bread Machine:*
- Pour the wet ingredients into the bread machine over the dry ingredients.
- *Mix in the Bread Machine:*

- Set the bread machine to the gluten-free setting and 2-pound loaf size.
- Press the start button to begin the mixing and kneading process.
- ***Pause and Add Mix-Ins:***
- When the machine signals the addition of mix-ins (usually indicated by a beep), add sunflower seeds.
- ***Complete the Cycle:***
- Allow the machine to run through the entire cycle.
- ***Cool and Slice:***
- After the cycle is complete, wait for 10 minutes before carefully removing the bread from the pan.
- Afterwards, transfer the bread to a wire rack and ensure it cools down completely before proceeding with slicing.

Nutritional Information (per slice, calculated for 16 slices):

- Calories: 120
- Protein: 3.5g
- Fat: 4.5g
- Carbs: 15g
- Fiber: 2g
- Sugars: 1.5g

40.   Sorghum & Date Bread

Ingredients:

- 1 1/2 cups sorghum flour
- 1/2 cup almond flour
- 1/4 cup chopped dates
- 2 teaspoons active dry yeast
- 1 teaspoon cinnamon
- 1 tablespoon maple syrup
- 4 large Flaxseed eggs
- 1 cup warm almond milk
- 1/4 cup coconut oil

Instructions:

- *Combine in the Bread Machine:*
- Place sorghum flour, almond flour, chopped dates, yeast, and cinnamon into the bread machine.
- *Prepare Wet Ingredients:*
- In a separate bowl, combine maple syrup, Flaxseed eggs, warm almond milk, and melted coconut oil.
- *Add Wet Ingredients to the Bread Machine:*
- Pour the wet ingredients into the bread machine over the dry ingredients.
- *Mix in the Bread Machine:*

- Set the bread machine to the gluten-free setting and 2-pound loaf size.
- Press the start button to begin the mixing and kneading process.
- ***Pause and Add Mix-Ins:***
- When the machine signals the addition of mix-ins (usually indicated by a beep), add chopped dates.
- ***Complete the Cycle:***
- Allow the machine to run through the entire cycle.
- ***Cool and Slice:***
- After the cycle is complete, wait for 10 minutes before carefully removing the bread from the pan.
- Afterwards, transfer the bread to a wire rack and ensure it cools down completely before proceeding with slicing.

Nutritional Information (per slice, calculated for 16 slices):

- Calories: 120
- Protein: 3.5g
- Fat: 4.5g
- Carbs: 15g
- Fiber: 2g
- Sugars: 1.5g

41.Chickpea & Currant Bread

Ingredients:

- 1 1/2 cups chickpea flour
- 1/2 cup sorghum flour
- 1/4 cup currants
- 2 teaspoons active dry yeast
- 1 teaspoon salt
- 1 tablespoon honey
- 3 large Flaxseed eggs
- 1 1/4 cups warm water
- 1/4 cup olive oil

Instructions:

- *Combine in the Bread Machine:*
- Place chickpea flour, sorghum flour, currants, yeast, and salt into the bread machine.
- *Prepare Wet Ingredients:*
- In a separate bowl, whisk together honey, Flaxseed eggs, warm water, and olive oil.
- *Add Wet Ingredients to the Bread Machine:*
- Pour the wet ingredients into the bread machine over the dry ingredients.
- *Mix in the Bread Machine:*

- Set the bread machine to the gluten-free setting and 2-pound loaf size.
- Press the start button to begin the mixing and kneading process.
- ***Pause and Add Mix-Ins:***
- When the machine signals the addition of mix-ins (usually indicated by a beep), add currants.
- ***Complete the Cycle:***
- Allow the machine to run through the entire cycle.
- ***Cool and Slice:***
- After the cycle is complete, wait for 10 minutes before carefully removing the bread from the pan.
- Afterwards, transfer the bread to a wire rack and ensure it cools down completely before proceeding with slicing.

Nutritional Information (per slice, calculated for 16 slices):

- Calories: 120
- Protein: 3.5g
- Fat: 4.5g
- Carbs: 15g
- Fiber: 2g
- Sugars: 2g

Ingredients:

- 1 1/2 cups pumpkin seed flour
- 1/2 cup almond flour
- 1/4 cup dried cranberries
- 2 teaspoons active dry yeast
- 1 teaspoon cinnamon
- 1 tablespoon maple syrup
- 4 large Flaxseed eggs
- 1 cup warm almond milk
- 1/4 cup coconut oil

Instructions:

- ***Combine in the Bread Machine:***
- Place pumpkin seed flour, almond flour, dried cranberries, yeast, and cinnamon into the bread machine.
- ***Prepare Wet Ingredients:***
- In a separate bowl, whisk together maple syrup, Flaxseed eggs, warm almond milk, and melted coconut oil.
- ***Add Wet Ingredients to the Bread Machine:***
- Pour the wet ingredients into the bread machine over the dry ingredients.
- ***Mix in the Bread Machine:***

- Set the bread machine to the gluten-free setting and 2-pound loaf size.
- Press the start button to begin the mixing and kneading process.
- *Pause and Add Mix-Ins:*
- When the machine signals the addition of mix-ins (usually indicated by a beep), add dried cranberries.
- *Complete the Cycle:*
- Allow the machine to run through the entire cycle.
- *Cool and Slice:*
- After the cycle is complete, wait for 10 minutes before carefully removing the bread from the pan.
- Afterwards, transfer the bread to a wire rack and ensure it cools down completely before proceeding with slicing.

Nutritional Information (per slice, calculated for 16 slices):

- Calories: 130
- Protein: 4.5g
- Fat: 6g
- Carbs: 16g
- Fiber: 2.5g
- Sugars: 2.5g

Ingredients:

- 1 1/2 cups amaranth flour
- 1/2 cup almond flour
- 1/4 cup chopped dates
- 2 teaspoons active dry yeast
- 1 teaspoon salt
- 1 tablespoon honey
- 3 large Flaxseed eggs
- 1 1/4 cups warm water
- 1/4 cup olive oil

Instructions:

- *Combine in the Bread Machine:*
- Place amaranth flour, almond flour, chopped dates, yeast, and salt into the bread machine.
- *Prepare Wet Ingredients:*
- In a separate bowl, whisk together honey, Flaxseed eggs, warm water, and olive oil.
- *Add Wet Ingredients to the Bread Machine:*
- Pour the wet ingredients into the bread machine over the dry ingredients.
- *Mix in the Bread Machine:*

- Set the bread machine to the gluten-free setting and 2-pound loaf size.
- Press the start button to begin the mixing and kneading process.
- ***Pause and Add Mix-Ins:***
- When the machine signals the addition of mix-ins (usually indicated by a beep), add chopped dates.
- ***Complete the Cycle:***
- Allow the machine to run through the entire cycle.
- ***Cool and Slice:***
- After the cycle is complete, wait for 10 minutes before carefully removing the bread from the pan.
- Afterwards, transfer the bread to a wire rack and ensure it cools down completely before proceeding with slicing.

Nutritional Information (per slice, calculated for 16 slices):

- Calories: 140
- Protein: 5g
- Fat: 7g
- Carbs: 16g
- Fiber: 2.5g
- Sugars: 2.5g

Ingredients:

- 1 1/2 cups flaxseed meal
- 1/2 cup almond flour
- 1/4 cup dried blueberries
- 2 teaspoons active dry yeast
- 1 teaspoon cinnamon
- 1 tablespoon maple syrup
- 4 large Flaxseed eggs
- 1 cup warm almond milk
- 1/4 cup coconut oil

Instructions:

- ***Combine in the Bread Machine:***
- Place flaxseed meal, almond flour, dried blueberries, yeast, and cinnamon into the bread machine.
- ***Prepare Wet Ingredients:***
- In a separate bowl, whisk together maple syrup, Flaxseed eggs, warm almond milk, and melted coconut oil.
- ***Add Wet Ingredients to the Bread Machine:***
- Pour the wet ingredients into the bread machine over the dry ingredients.
- ***Mix in the Bread Machine:***

- Set the bread machine to the gluten-free setting and 2-pound loaf size.
- Press the start button to begin the mixing and kneading process.
- ***Pause and Add Mix-Ins:***
- When the machine signals the addition of mix-ins (usually indicated by a beep), add dried blueberries.
- ***Complete the Cycle:***
- Allow the machine to run through the entire cycle.
- ***Cool and Slice:***
- After the cycle is complete, wait for 10 minutes before carefully removing the bread from the pan.
- Afterwards, transfer the bread to a wire rack and ensure it cools down completely before proceeding with slicing.

Nutritional Information (per slice, calculated for 16 slices):

- Calories: 140
- Protein: 5g
- Fat: 7g
- Carbs: 16g
- Fiber: 2.5g
- Sugars: 2.5g

Ingredients:

- 1 1/2 cups buckwheat flour
- 1/2 cup walnut flour
- 1/4 cup chopped walnuts
- 2 teaspoons active dry yeast
- 1 teaspoon salt
- 1 tablespoon honey
- 3 large Flaxseed eggs
- 1 1/4 cups warm water
- 1/4 cup olive oil

Instructions:

- ***Combine in the Bread Machine:***
- Place buckwheat flour, walnut flour, chopped walnuts, yeast, and salt into the bread machine.
- ***Prepare Wet Ingredients:***
- In a separate bowl, whisk together honey, Flaxseed eggs, warm water, and olive oil.
- ***Add Wet Ingredients to the Bread Machine:***
- Pour the wet ingredients into the bread machine over the dry ingredients.
- ***Mix in the Bread Machine:***

- Set the bread machine to the gluten-free setting and 2-pound loaf size.
- Press the start button to begin the mixing and kneading process.
- ***Pause and Add Mix-Ins:***
- When the machine signals the addition of mix-ins (usually indicated by a beep), add chopped walnuts.
- ***Complete the Cycle:***
- Allow the machine to run through the entire cycle.
- ***Cool and Slice:***
- After the cycle is complete, wait for 10 minutes before carefully removing the bread from the pan.
- Afterwards, transfer the bread to a wire rack and ensure it cools down completely before proceeding with slicing.

Nutritional Information (per slice, calculated for 16 slices):

- Calories: 140
- Protein: 5g
- Fat: 7g
- Carbs: 16g
- Fiber: 3g
- Sugars: 2g

46.   Coconut Flour & Pineapple Bread

Ingredients:

- 1 1/2 cups coconut flour
- 1/2 cup almond flour
- 1/4 cup dried pineapple, chopped
- 2 teaspoons active dry yeast
- 1 teaspoon salt
- 1 tablespoon maple syrup
- 4 large Flaxseed eggs
- 1 cup warm water
- 1/4 cup coconut oil

Instructions:

- ***Combine in the Bread Machine:***
- Place coconut flour, almond flour, dried pineapple, yeast, and salt into the bread machine.
- ***Prepare Wet Ingredients:***
- In a separate bowl, whisk together maple syrup, Flaxseed eggs, warm water, and melted coconut oil.
- ***Add Wet Ingredients to the Bread Machine:***
- Pour the wet ingredients into the bread machine over the dry ingredients.
- ***Mix in the Bread Machine:***

- Set the bread machine to the gluten-free setting and 2-pound loaf size.
- Press the start button to begin the mixing and kneading process.
- ***Pause and Add Mix-Ins:***
- When the machine signals the addition of mix-ins (usually indicated by a beep), add dried pineapple.
- ***Complete the Cycle:***
- Allow the machine to run through the entire cycle.
- ***Cool and Slice:***
- After the cycle is complete, wait for 10 minutes before carefully removing the bread from the pan.
- Afterwards, transfer the bread to a wire rack and ensure it cools down completely before proceeding with slicing.

Nutritional Information (per slice, calculated for 16 slices):

- Calories: 130
- Protein: 4.5g
- Fat: 6g
- Carbs: 16g
- Fiber: 2.5g
- Sugars: 2.5g

Ingredients:

- 1 1/2 cups hazelnut flour
- 1/2 cup almond flour
- 1/4 cup chopped dried figs
- 2 teaspoons active dry yeast
- 1 teaspoon cinnamon
- 1 tablespoon honey
- 3 large Flaxseed eggs
- 1 1/4 cups warm water
- 1/4 cup olive oil

Instructions:

- *Combine in the Bread Machine:*
- Place hazelnut flour, almond flour, chopped dried figs, yeast, and cinnamon into the bread machine.
- *Prepare Wet Ingredients:*
- In a separate bowl, whisk together honey, Flaxseed eggs, warm water, and olive oil.
- *Add Wet Ingredients to the Bread Machine:*
- Pour the wet ingredients into the bread machine over the dry ingredients.
- *Mix in the Bread Machine:*

- Set the bread machine to the gluten-free setting and 2-pound loaf size.
- Press the start button to begin the mixing and kneading process.
- ***Pause and Add Mix-Ins:***
- When the machine signals the addition of mix-ins (usually indicated by a beep), add chopped dried figs.
- ***Complete the Cycle:***
- Allow the machine to run through the entire cycle.
- ***Cool and Slice:***
- After the cycle is complete, wait for 10 minutes before carefully removing the bread from the pan.
- Afterwards, transfer the bread to a wire rack and ensure it cools down completely before proceeding with slicing.

Nutritional Information (per slice, calculated for 16 slices):

- Calories: 140
- Protein: 5g
- Fat: 7g
- Carbs: 16g
- Fiber: 2.5g
- Sugars: 2.5g

Ingredients:

- 1 1/2 cups almond flour
- 1/2 cup coconut flour
- 1/4 cup dried cranberries
- 2 teaspoons active dry yeast
- 1 teaspoon cinnamon
- 1 tablespoon maple syrup
- 4 large Flaxseed eggs
- 1 cup warm almond milk
- 1/4 cup coconut oil

Instructions:

- ***Combine in the Bread Machine:***
- Place almond flour, coconut flour, dried cranberries, yeast, and cinnamon into the bread machine.
- ***Prepare Wet Ingredients:***
- In a separate bowl, whisk together maple syrup, Flaxseed eggs, warm almond milk, and melted coconut oil.
- ***Add Wet Ingredients to the Bread Machine:***
- Pour the wet ingredients into the bread machine over the dry ingredients.
- ***Mix in the Bread Machine:***

- Set the bread machine to the gluten-free setting and 2-pound loaf size.
- Press the start button to begin the mixing and kneading process.
- ***Pause and Add Mix-Ins:***
- When the machine signals the addition of mix-ins (usually indicated by a beep), add dried cranberries.
- ***Complete the Cycle:***
- Allow the machine to run through the entire cycle.
- ***Cool and Slice:***
- After the cycle is complete, wait for 10 minutes before carefully removing the bread from the pan.
- Afterwards, transfer the bread to a wire rack and ensure it cools down completely before proceeding with slicing.

Nutritional Information (per slice, calculated for 16 slices):

- Calories: 130
- Protein: 4.5g
- Fat: 7g
- Carbs: 16g
- Fiber: 2.5g
- Sugars: 2.5g

49.   Pistachio & Apricot Bread

Ingredients:

- 1 1/2 cups pistachio flour
- 1/2 cup almond flour
- 1/4 cup chopped dried apricots
- 2 teaspoons active dry yeast
- 1 teaspoon salt
- 1 tablespoon honey
- 3 large Flaxseed eggs
- 1 1/4 cups warm water
- 1/4 cup olive oil

Instructions:

- ***Combine in the Bread Machine:***
- Place pistachio flour, almond flour, chopped dried apricots, yeast, and salt into the bread machine.
- ***Prepare Wet Ingredients:***
- In a separate bowl, whisk together honey, Flaxseed eggs, warm water, and olive oil.
- ***Add Wet Ingredients to the Bread Machine:***
- Pour the wet ingredients into the bread machine over the dry ingredients.
- ***Mix in the Bread Machine:***

- Set the bread machine to the gluten-free setting and 2-pound loaf size.
- Press the start button to begin the mixing and kneading process.
- *Pause and Add Mix-Ins:*
- When the machine signals the addition of mix-ins (usually indicated by a beep), add chopped dried apricots.
- *Complete the Cycle:*
- Allow the machine to run through the entire cycle.
- *Cool and Slice:*
- After the cycle is complete, wait for 10 minutes before carefully removing the bread from the pan.
- Afterwards, transfer the bread to a wire rack and ensure it cools down completely before proceeding with slicing.

Nutritional Information (per slice, calculated for 16 slices):

- Calories: 140
- Protein: 5g
- Fat: 7g
- Carbs: 16g
- Fiber: 3g
- Sugars: 2g

50.   Quinoa & Raspberry Bread

Ingredients:

- 1 1/2 cups quinoa flour
- 1/2 cup almond flour
- 1/4 cup freeze-dried raspberries, crushed
- 2 teaspoons active dry yeast
- 1 teaspoon cinnamon
- 1 tablespoon maple syrup
- 4 large Flaxseed eggs
- 1 cup warm almond milk
- 1/4 cup coconut oil

Instructions:

- ***Combine in the Bread Machine:***
- Place quinoa flour, almond flour, crushed freeze-dried raspberries, yeast, and cinnamon into the bread machine.
- ***Prepare Wet Ingredients:***
- In a separate bowl, whisk together maple syrup, Flaxseed eggs, warm almond milk, and melted coconut oil.
- ***Add Wet Ingredients to the Bread Machine:***
- Pour the wet ingredients into the bread machine over the dry ingredients.
- ***Mix in the Bread Machine:***

- Set the bread machine to the gluten-free setting and 2-pound loaf size.
- Press the start button to begin the mixing and kneading process.
- ***Pause and Add Mix-Ins:***
- When the machine signals the addition of mix-ins (usually indicated by a beep), add crushed freeze-dried raspberries.
- ***Complete the Cycle:***
- Allow the machine to run through the entire cycle.
- ***Cool and Slice:***
- After the cycle is complete, wait for 10 minutes before carefully removing the bread from the pan.
- Afterwards, transfer the bread to a wire rack and ensure it cools down completely before proceeding with slicing.

Nutritional Information (per slice, calculated for 16 slices):

- Calories: 130
- Protein: 4.5g
- Fat: 6g
- Carbs: 16g
- Fiber: 2.5g
- Sugars: 2.5g

51. Sesame & Date Bread

Ingredients:

- 1 1/2 cups sesame flour
- 1/2 cup almond flour
- 1/4 cup chopped dates
- 2 teaspoons active dry yeast
- 1 teaspoon salt
- 1 tablespoon honey
- 3 large Flaxseed eggs
- 1 1/4 cups warm water
- 1/4 cup olive oil

Instructions:

- *Combine in the Bread Machine:*
- Place sesame flour, almond flour, chopped dates, yeast, and salt into the bread machine.
- *Prepare Wet Ingredients:*
- In a separate bowl, whisk together honey, Flaxseed eggs, warm water, and olive oil.
- *Add Wet Ingredients to the Bread Machine:*
- Pour the wet ingredients into the bread machine over the dry ingredients.
- *Mix in the Bread Machine:*

- Set the bread machine to the gluten-free setting and 2-pound loaf size.
- Press the start button to begin the mixing and kneading process.
- ***Pause and Add Mix-Ins:***
- When the machine signals the addition of mix-ins (usually indicated by a beep), add chopped dates.
- ***Complete the Cycle:***
- Allow the machine to run through the entire cycle.
- ***Cool and Slice:***
- After the cycle is complete, wait for 10 minutes before carefully removing the bread from the pan.
- Afterwards, transfer the bread to a wire rack and ensure it cools down completely before proceeding with slicing.

Nutritional Information (per slice, calculated for 16 slices):

- Calories: 140
- Protein: 5g
- Fat: 7g
- Carbs: 16g
- Fiber: 2.5g
- Sugars: 2.5g

Ingredients:

- 1 1/2 cups sunflower seed flour
- 1/2 cup almond flour
- 1/4 cup dried blueberries
- 2 teaspoons active dry yeast
- 1 teaspoon cinnamon
- 1 tablespoon maple syrup
- 4 large Flaxseed eggs
- 1 cup warm almond milk
- 1/4 cup coconut oil

Instructions:

- *Combine in the Bread Machine:*
- Place sunflower seed flour, almond flour, dried blueberries, yeast, and cinnamon into the bread machine.
- *Prepare Wet Ingredients:*
- In a separate bowl, whisk together maple syrup, Flaxseed eggs, warm almond milk, and melted coconut oil.
- *Add Wet Ingredients to the Bread Machine:*
- Pour the wet ingredients into the bread machine over the dry ingredients.
- *Mix in the Bread Machine:*

- Set the bread machine to the gluten-free setting and 2-pound loaf size.
- Press the start button to begin the mixing and kneading process.
- *Pause and Add Mix-Ins:*
- When the machine signals the addition of mix-ins (usually indicated by a beep), add dried blueberries.
- *Complete the Cycle:*
- Allow the machine to run through the entire cycle.
- *Cool and Slice:*
- After the cycle is complete, wait for 10 minutes before carefully removing the bread from the pan.
- Afterwards, transfer the bread to a wire rack and ensure it cools down completely before proceeding with slicing.

Nutritional Information (per slice, calculated for 16 slices):

- Calories: 140
- Protein: 5g
- Fat: 7g
- Carbs: 16g
- Fiber: 2.5g
- Sugars: 2.5g

Ingredients:

- 1 1/2 cups almond flour
- 1/2 cup coconut flour
- 1/4 cup dried cranberries
- 2 teaspoons active dry yeast
- 1 teaspoon cinnamon
- 1 tablespoon maple syrup
- 4 large Flaxseed eggs
- 1 cup warm almond milk
- 1/4 cup coconut oil

Instructions:

- *Combine in the Bread Machine:*
- Place almond flour, coconut flour, dried cranberries, yeast, and cinnamon into the bread machine.
- *Prepare Wet Ingredients:*
- In a separate bowl, whisk together maple syrup, Flaxseed eggs, warm almond milk, and melted coconut oil.
- *Add Wet Ingredients to the Bread Machine:*
- Pour the wet ingredients into the bread machine over the dry ingredients.
- *Mix in the Bread Machine:*

- Set the bread machine to the gluten-free setting and 2-pound loaf size.
- Press the start button to begin the mixing and kneading process.
- ***Pause and Add Mix-Ins:***
- When the machine signals the addition of mix-ins (usually indicated by a beep), add dried cranberries.
- ***Complete the Cycle:***
- Allow the machine to run through the entire cycle.
- ***Cool and Slice:***
- After the cycle is complete, wait for 10 minutes before carefully removing the bread from the pan.
- Afterwards, transfer the bread to a wire rack and ensure it cools down completely before proceeding with slicing.

Nutritional Information (per slice, calculated for 16 slices):

- Calories: 130
- Protein: 4.5g
- Fat: 6g
- Carbs: 16g
- Fiber: 2.5g
- Sugars: 2.5g

Ingredients:

- 1 1/2 cups pumpkin seed flour
- 1/2 cup almond flour
- 1/4 cup chopped dried figs
- 2 teaspoons active dry yeast
- 1 teaspoon cinnamon
- 1 tablespoon maple syrup
- 4 large Flaxseed eggs
- 1 cup warm almond milk
- 1/4 cup coconut oil

Instructions:

- *Combine in the Bread Machine:*
- Place pumpkin seed flour, almond flour, chopped dried figs, yeast, and cinnamon into the bread machine.
- *Prepare Wet Ingredients:*
- In a separate bowl, whisk together maple syrup, Flaxseed eggs, warm almond milk, and melted coconut oil.
- *Add Wet Ingredients to the Bread Machine:*
- Pour the wet ingredients into the bread machine over the dry ingredients.
- *Mix in the Bread Machine:*

- Set the bread machine to the gluten-free setting and 2-pound loaf size.
- Press the start button to begin the mixing and kneading process.
- *Pause and Add Mix-Ins:*
- When the machine signals the addition of mix-ins (usually indicated by a beep), add chopped dried figs.
- *Complete the Cycle:*
- Allow the machine to run through the entire cycle.
- *Cool and Slice:*
- After the cycle is complete, wait for 10 minutes before carefully removing the bread from the pan.
- Afterwards, transfer the bread to a wire rack and ensure it cools down completely before proceeding with slicing.

Nutritional Information (per slice, calculated for 16 slices):

- Calories: 130
- Protein: 4.5g
- Fat: 6g
- Carbs: 16g
- Fiber: 2.5g
- Sugars: 2.5g

Ingredients:

- 1 1/2 cups sunflower seed flour
- 1/2 cup almond flour
- 1/4 cup chopped dates
- 2 teaspoons active dry yeast
- 1 teaspoon salt
- 1 tablespoon honey
- 3 large Flaxseed eggs
- 1 1/4 cups warm water
- 1/4 cup olive oil

Instructions:

- *Combine in the Bread Machine:*
- Place sunflower seed flour, almond flour, chopped dates, yeast, and salt into the bread machine.
- *Prepare Wet Ingredients:*
- In a separate bowl, whisk together honey, Flaxseed eggs, warm water, and olive oil.
- *Add Wet Ingredients to the Bread Machine:*
- Pour the wet ingredients into the bread machine over the dry ingredients.
- *Mix in the Bread Machine:*

- Set the bread machine to the gluten-free setting and 2-pound loaf size.
- Press the start button to begin the mixing and kneading process.
- *Pause and Add Mix-Ins:*
- When the machine signals the addition of mix-ins (usually indicated by a beep), add chopped dates.
- *Complete the Cycle:*
- Allow the machine to run through the entire cycle.
- *Cool and Slice:*
- After the cycle is complete, wait for 10 minutes before carefully removing the bread from the pan.
- Afterwards, transfer the bread to a wire rack and ensure it cools down completely before proceeding with slicing.

Nutritional Information (per slice, calculated for 16 slices):

- Calories: 140
- Protein: 5g
- Fat: 7g
- Carbs: 16g
- Fiber: 3g
- Sugars: 2g

56.   Amaranth & Blueberry Bread

Ingredients:

- 1 1/2 cups amaranth flour
- 1/2 cup almond flour
- 1/4 cup dried blueberries
- 2 teaspoons active dry yeast
- 1 teaspoon cinnamon
- 1 tablespoon maple syrup
- 4 large Flaxseed eggs
- 1 cup warm almond milk
- 1/4 cup coconut oil

Instructions:

- ***Combine in the Bread Machine:***
- Place amaranth flour, almond flour, dried blueberries, yeast, and cinnamon into the bread machine.
- ***Prepare Wet Ingredients:***
- In a separate bowl, whisk together maple syrup, Flaxseed eggs, warm almond milk, and melted coconut oil.
- ***Add Wet Ingredients to the Bread Machine:***
- Pour the wet ingredients into the bread machine over the dry ingredients.
- ***Mix in the Bread Machine:***

- Set the bread machine to the gluten-free setting and 2-pound loaf size.
- Press the start button to begin the mixing and kneading process.
- ***Pause and Add Mix-Ins:***
- When the machine signals the addition of mix-ins (usually indicated by a beep), add dried blueberries.
- ***Complete the Cycle:***
- Allow the machine to run through the entire cycle.
- ***Cool and Slice:***
- After the cycle is complete, wait for 10 minutes before carefully removing the bread from the pan.
- Afterwards, transfer the bread to a wire rack and ensure it cools down completely before proceeding with slicing.

Nutritional Information (per slice, calculated for 16 slices):

- Calories: 130
- Protein: 4.5g
- Fat: 6g
- Carbs: 16g
- Fiber: 2.5g
- Sugars: 2.5g

57.Pumpkin Seed & Apricot Bread

Ingredients:

- 1 1/2 cups pumpkin seed flour
- 1/2 cup almond flour
- 1/4 cup chopped dried apricots
- 2 teaspoons active dry yeast
- 1 teaspoon cinnamon
- 1 tablespoon honey
- 3 large Flaxseed eggs
- 1 1/4 cups warm water
- 1/4 cup olive oil

Instructions:

- *Combine in the Bread Machine:*
- Place pumpkin seed flour, almond flour, chopped dried apricots, yeast, and cinnamon into the bread machine.
- *Prepare Wet Ingredients:*
- In a separate bowl, whisk together honey, Flaxseed eggs, warm water, and olive oil.
- *Add Wet Ingredients to the Bread Machine:*
- Pour the wet ingredients into the bread machine over the dry ingredients.
- *Mix in the Bread Machine:*

- Set the bread machine to the gluten-free setting and 2-pound loaf size.
- Press the start button to begin the mixing and kneading process.
- ***Pause and Add Mix-Ins:***
- When the machine signals the addition of mix-ins (usually indicated by a beep), add chopped dried apricots.
- ***Complete the Cycle:***
- Allow the machine to run through the entire cycle.
- ***Cool and Slice:***
- After the cycle is complete, wait for 10 minutes before carefully removing the bread from the pan.
- Afterwards, transfer the bread to a wire rack and ensure it cools down completely before proceeding with slicing.

Nutritional Information (per slice, calculated for 16 slices):

- Calories: 140
- Protein: 5g
- Fat: 7g
- Carbs: 16g
- Fiber: 3g
- Sugars: 2g

Ingredients:

- 1 1/2 cups flaxseed meal
- 1/2 cup almond flour
- 1/4 cup dried cranberries
- 2 teaspoons active dry yeast
- 1 teaspoon cinnamon
- 1 tablespoon maple syrup
- 4 large Flaxseed eggs
- 1 cup warm almond milk
- 1/4 cup coconut oil

Instructions:

- *Combine in the Bread Machine:*
- Place flaxseed meal, almond flour, dried cranberries, yeast, and cinnamon into the bread machine.
- *Prepare Wet Ingredients:*
- In a separate bowl, whisk together maple syrup, Flaxseed eggs, warm almond milk, and melted coconut oil.
- *Add Wet Ingredients to the Bread Machine:*
- Pour the wet ingredients into the bread machine over the dry ingredients.
- *Mix in the Bread Machine:*

- Set the bread machine to the gluten-free setting and 2-pound loaf size.
- Press the start button to begin the mixing and kneading process.
- ***Pause and Add Mix-Ins:***
- When the machine signals the addition of mix-ins (usually indicated by a beep), add dried cranberries.
- ***Complete the Cycle:***
- Allow the machine to run through the entire cycle.
- ***Cool and Slice:***
- After the cycle is complete, wait for 10 minutes before carefully removing the bread from the pan.
- Afterwards, transfer the bread to a wire rack and ensure it cools down completely before proceeding with slicing.

Nutritional Information (per slice, calculated for 16 slices):

- Calories: 130
- Protein: 5g
- Fat: 7g
- Carbs: 16g
- Fiber: 3g
- Sugars: 2g

Ingredients:

- 1 1/2 cups chia seed flour
- 1/2 cup almond flour
- 1/4 cup dried mango, chopped
- 2 teaspoons active dry yeast
- 1 teaspoon cinnamon
- 1 tablespoon honey
- 3 large Flaxseed eggs
- 1 1/4 cups warm water
- 1/4 cup olive oil

Instructions:

Combine in the Bread Machine:
- Place chia seed flour, almond flour, chopped dried mango, yeast, and cinnamon into the bread machine.
- **Prepare Wet Ingredients:**
- In a separate bowl, whisk together honey, Flaxseed eggs, warm water, and olive oil.
- **Add Wet Ingredients to the Bread Machine:**
- Pour the wet ingredients into the bread machine over the dry ingredients.
- **Mix in the Bread Machine:**
- Set the bread machine to the gluten-free setting and 2-pound loaf size.

- Press the start button to begin the mixing and kneading process.
- ***Pause and Add Mix-Ins:***
- When the machine signals the addition of mix-ins (usually indicated by a beep), add chopped dried mango.
- ***Complete the Cycle:***
- Allow the machine to run through the entire cycle.
- ***Cool and Slice:***
- After the cycle is complete, wait for 10 minutes before carefully removing the bread from the pan.
- Afterwards, transfer the bread to a wire rack and ensure it cools down completely before proceeding with slicing.

Nutritional Information (per slice, calculated for 16 slices):

- Calories: 140
- Protein: 5g
- Fat: 7g
- Carbs: 16g
- Fiber: 3g
- Sugars: 2g

Ingredients:

- 1 1/2 cups buckwheat flour
- 1/2 cup almond flour
- 1/4 cup dried cherries
- 2 teaspoons active dry yeast
- 1 teaspoon salt
- 1 tablespoon honey
- 3 large Flaxseed eggs
- 1 1/4 cups warm water
- 1/4 cup olive oil

Instructions:

- *Combine in the Bread Machine:*
- Place buckwheat flour, almond flour, dried cherries, yeast, and salt into the bread machine.
- *Prepare Wet Ingredients:*
- In a separate bowl, whisk together honey, Flaxseed eggs, warm water, and olive oil.
- *Add Wet Ingredients to the Bread Machine:*
- Pour the wet ingredients into the bread machine over the dry ingredients.
- *Mix in the Bread Machine:*

- Set the bread machine to the gluten-free setting and 2-pound loaf size.
- Press the start button to begin the mixing and kneading process.
- ***Pause and Add Mix-Ins:***
- When the machine signals the addition of mix-ins (usually indicated by a beep), add dried cherries.
- ***Complete the Cycle:***
- Allow the machine to run through the entire cycle.
- ***Cool and Slice:***
- After the cycle is complete, wait for 10 minutes before carefully removing the bread from the pan.
- Afterwards, transfer the bread to a wire rack and ensure it cools down completely before proceeding with slicing.

Nutritional Information (per slice, calculated for 16 slices):

- Calories: 140
- Protein: 5g
- Fat: 7g
- Carbs: 16g
- Fiber: 3g
- Sugars: 2g

61. Coconut Flour & Blackberry Bread

Ingredients:

- 1 1/2 cups coconut flour
- 1/2 cup almond flour
- 1/4 cup dried blackberries
- 2 teaspoons active dry yeast
- 1 teaspoon cinnamon
- 1 tablespoon honey
- 3 large Flaxseed eggs
- 1 1/4 cups warm water
- 1/4 cup olive oil

Instructions:

- *Combine in the Bread Machine:*
- Place coconut flour, almond flour, dried blackberries, yeast, and cinnamon into the bread machine.
- *Prepare Wet Ingredients:*
- In a separate bowl, whisk together honey, Flaxseed eggs, warm water, and olive oil.
- *Add Wet Ingredients to the Bread Machine:*
- Pour the wet ingredients into the bread machine over the dry ingredients.
- *Mix in the Bread Machine:*

- Set the bread machine to the gluten-free setting and 2-pound loaf size.
- Press the start button to begin the mixing and kneading process.
- *Pause and Add Mix-Ins:*
- When the machine signals the addition of mix-ins (usually indicated by a beep), add dried blackberries.
- *Complete the Cycle:*
- Allow the machine to run through the entire cycle.
- *Cool and Slice:*
- After the cycle is complete, wait for 10 minutes before carefully removing the bread from the pan.
- Afterwards, transfer the bread to a wire rack and ensure it cools down completely before proceeding with slicing.

Nutritional Information (per slice, calculated for 16 slices):

- Calories: 130
- Protein: 4.5g
- Fat: 6g
- Carbs: 14g
- Fiber: 3g
- Sugars: 2g

62. Quinoa & Cranberry Bread

Ingredients:

- 1 1/2 cups quinoa flour
- 1/2 cup almond flour
- 1/4 cup dried cranberries
- 2 teaspoons active dry yeast
- 1 teaspoon cinnamon
- 1 tablespoon maple syrup
- 4 large Flaxseed eggs
- 1 cup warm almond milk
- 1/4 cup coconut oil

Instructions:

- ***Combine in the Bread Machine:***
- Place quinoa flour, almond flour, dried cranberries, yeast, and cinnamon into the bread machine.
- ***Prepare Wet Ingredients:***
- In a separate bowl, whisk together maple syrup, Flaxseed eggs, warm almond milk, and melted coconut oil.
- ***Add Wet Ingredients to the Bread Machine:***
- Pour the wet ingredients into the bread machine over the dry ingredients.
- ***Mix in the Bread Machine:***

- Set the bread machine to the gluten-free setting and 2-pound loaf size.
- Press the start button to begin the mixing and kneading process.
- ***Pause and Add Mix-Ins:***
- When the machine signals the addition of mix-ins (usually indicated by a beep), add dried cranberries.
- ***Complete the Cycle:***
- Allow the machine to run through the entire cycle.
- ***Cool and Slice:***
- After the cycle is complete, wait for 10 minutes before carefully removing the bread from the pan.
- Afterwards, transfer the bread to a wire rack and ensure it cools down completely before proceeding with slicing.

Nutritional Information (per slice, calculated for 16 slices):

- Calories: 130
- Protein: 4.5g
- Fat: 6g
- Carbs: 16g
- Fiber: 2.5g
- Sugars: 2.5g

Ingredients:

- 1 1/2 cups amaranth flour
- 1/2 cup almond flour
- 1/4 cup freeze-dried raspberries, crushed
- 2 teaspoons active dry yeast
- 1 teaspoon cinnamon
- 1 tablespoon honey
- 3 large Flaxseed eggs
- 1 1/4 cups warm water
- 1/4 cup olive oil

Instructions:

- *Combine in the Bread Machine:*
- Place amaranth flour, almond flour, crushed freeze-dried raspberries, yeast, and cinnamon into the bread machine.
- *Prepare Wet Ingredients:*
- In a separate bowl, whisk together honey, Flaxseed eggs, warm water, and olive oil.
- *Add Wet Ingredients to the Bread Machine:*
- Pour the wet ingredients into the bread machine over the dry ingredients.
- *Mix in the Bread Machine:*

- Set the bread machine to the gluten-free setting and 2-pound loaf size.
- Press the start button to begin the mixing and kneading process.
- ***Pause and Add Mix-Ins:***
- When the machine signals the addition of mix-ins (usually indicated by a beep), add crushed freeze-dried raspberries.
- ***Complete the Cycle:***
- Allow the machine to run through the entire cycle.
- ***Cool and Slice:***
- After the cycle is complete, wait for 10 minutes before carefully removing the bread from the pan.
- Afterwards, transfer the bread to a wire rack and ensure it cools down completely before proceeding with slicing.

Nutritional Information (per slice, calculated for 16 slices):

- Calories: 130
- Protein: 4.5g
- Fat: 6g
- Carbs: 16g
- Fiber: 2.5g
- Sugars: 2.5g

Ingredients:

- 1 1/2 cups flaxseed meal
- 1/2 cup almond flour
- 1/4 cup dried blackberries
- 2 teaspoons active dry yeast
- 1 teaspoon cinnamon
- 1 tablespoon honey
- 3 large Flaxseed eggs
- 1 1/4 cups warm water
- 1/4 cup olive oil

Instructions:

- *Combine in the Bread Machine:*
- Place flaxseed meal, almond flour, dried blackberries, yeast, and cinnamon into the bread machine.
- *Prepare Wet Ingredients:*
- In a separate bowl, whisk together honey, Flaxseed eggs, warm water, and olive oil.
- *Add Wet Ingredients to the Bread Machine:*
- Pour the wet ingredients into the bread machine over the dry ingredients.
- *Mix in the Bread Machine:*

- Set the bread machine to the gluten-free setting and 2-pound loaf size.
- Press the start button to begin the mixing and kneading process.
- *Pause and Add Mix-Ins:*
- When the machine signals the addition of mix-ins (usually indicated by a beep), add dried blackberries.
- *Complete the Cycle:*
- Allow the machine to run through the entire cycle.
- *Cool and Slice:*
- After the cycle is complete, wait for 10 minutes before carefully removing the bread from the pan.
- Afterwards, transfer the bread to a wire rack and ensure it cools down completely before proceeding with slicing.

Nutritional Values (per slice, based on 16 slices):

- Calories: 130
- Protein: 4.5g
- Fat: 6g
- Carbs: 16g
- Fiber: 2.5g
- Sugars: 2.5g

Ingredients:

- 1 1/2 cups sesame flour
- 1/2 cup almond flour
- 1/4 cup dried blueberries
- 2 teaspoons active dry yeast
- 1 teaspoon cinnamon
- 1 tablespoon maple syrup
- 4 large Flaxseed eggs
- 1 cup warm almond milk
- 1/4 cup coconut oil

Instructions:

- *Combine in the Bread Machine:*
- Place sesame flour, almond flour, dried blueberries, yeast, and cinnamon into the bread machine.
- *Prepare Wet Ingredients:*
- In a separate bowl, whisk together maple syrup, Flaxseed eggs, warm almond milk, and melted coconut oil.
- *Add Wet Ingredients to the Bread Machine:*
- Pour the wet ingredients into the bread machine over the dry ingredients.
- *Mix in the Bread Machine:*

- Set the bread machine to the gluten-free setting and 2-pound loaf size.
- Press the start button to begin the mixing and kneading process.
- ***Pause and Add Mix-Ins:***
- When the machine signals the addition of mix-ins (usually indicated by a beep), add dried blueberries.
- ***Complete the Cycle:***
- Allow the machine to run through the entire cycle.
- ***Cool and Slice:***
- After the cycle is complete, wait for 10 minutes before carefully removing the bread from the pan.
- Afterwards, transfer the bread to a wire rack and ensure it cools down completely before proceeding with slicing.

Nutritional Values (per slice, based on calculated for 16 slices):

- Calories: 140
- Protein: 5g
- Fat: 7g
- Carbs: 16g
- Fiber: 3g
- Sugars: 2g

Ingredients:

- 1 1/2 cups teff flour
- 1/2 cup almond flour
- 1/4 cup chopped dates
- 2 teaspoons active dry yeast
- 1 teaspoon cinnamon
- 1 tablespoon honey
- 3 large Flaxseed eggs
- 1 1/4 cups warm water
- 1/4 cup olive oil

Instructions:

- *Combine in the Bread Machine:*
- Place teff flour, almond flour, chopped dates, yeast, and cinnamon into the bread machine.
- *Prepare Wet Ingredients:*
- In a separate bowl, whisk together honey, Flaxseed eggs, warm water, and olive oil.
- *Add Wet Ingredients to the Bread Machine:*
- Pour the wet ingredients into the bread machine over the dry ingredients.
- *Mix in the Bread Machine:*

- Set the bread machine to the gluten-free setting and 2-pound loaf size.
- Press the start button to begin the mixing and kneading process.
- ***Pause and Add Mix-Ins:***
- When the machine signals the addition of mix-ins (usually indicated by a beep), add chopped dates.
- ***Complete the Cycle:***
- Allow the machine to run through the entire cycle.
- ***Cool and Slice:***
- After the cycle is complete, wait for 10 minutes before carefully removing the bread from the pan.
- Afterwards, transfer the bread to a wire rack and ensure it cools down completely before proceeding with slicing.

Nutritional Values (per slice, based on 16 slices):

- Calories: 140
- Protein: 5g
- Fat: 7g
- Carbs: 16g
- Fiber: 3g
- Sugars: 2g

Ingredients:

- 1 1/2 cups buckwheat flour
- 1/2 cup almond flour
- 1/4 cup chopped dried apricots
- 2 teaspoons active dry yeast
- 1 teaspoon salt
- 1 tablespoon honey
- 3 large Flaxseed eggs
- 1 1/4 cups warm water
- 1/4 cup olive oil

Instructions:

- ***Combine in the Bread Machine:***

- Place buckwheat flour, almond flour, chopped dried apricots, yeast, and salt into the bread machine.
- ***Prepare Wet Ingredients:***
- In a separate bowl, whisk together honey, Flaxseed eggs, warm water, and olive oil.
- ***Add Wet Ingredients to the Bread Machine:***
- Pour the wet ingredients into the bread machine over the dry ingredients.
- ***Mix in the Bread Machine:***

- Set the bread machine to the gluten-free setting and 2-pound loaf size.
- Press the start button to begin the mixing and kneading process.
- *Pause and Add Mix-Ins:*
- When the machine signals the addition of mix-ins (usually indicated by a beep), add chopped dried apricots.
- *Complete the Cycle:*
- Allow the machine to run through the entire cycle.
- *Cool and Slice:*
- After the cycle is complete, wait for 10 minutes before carefully removing the bread from the pan.
- Afterwards, transfer the bread to a wire rack and ensure it cools down completely before proceeding with slicing.

Nutritional Values (per slice, based on 16 slices):

- Calories: 140
- Protein: 5g
- Fat: 7g
- Carbs: 16g
- Fiber: 3g
- Sugars: 2g

68. Sorghum & Blackberry Bread

Ingredients:

- 1 1/2 cups sorghum flour
- 1/2 cup almond flour
- 1/4 cup dried blackberries
- 2 teaspoons active dry yeast
- 1 teaspoon cinnamon
- 1 tablespoon honey
- 3 large Flaxseed eggs
- 1 1/4 cups warm water
- 1/4 cup olive oil

Instructions:

- *Combine in the Bread Machine:*
- Place sorghum flour, almond flour, dried blackberries, yeast, and cinnamon into the bread machine.
- *Prepare Wet Ingredients:*
- In a separate bowl, whisk together honey, Flaxseed eggs, warm water, and olive oil.
- *Add Wet Ingredients to the Bread Machine:*
- Pour the wet ingredients into the bread machine over the dry ingredients.
- *Mix in the Bread Machine:*

- Set the bread machine to the gluten-free setting and 2-pound loaf size.
- Press the start button to begin the mixing and kneading process.
- *Pause and Add Mix-Ins:*
- When the machine signals the addition of mix-ins (usually indicated by a beep), add dried blackberries.
- *Complete the Cycle:*
- Allow the machine to run through the entire cycle.
- *Cool and Slice:*
- After the cycle is complete, wait for 10 minutes before carefully removing the bread from the pan.
- Afterwards, transfer the bread to a wire rack and ensure it cools down completely before proceeding with slicing.

Nutritional Information (per slice, calculated for 16 slices):

- Calories: 130
- Protein: 4.5g
- Fat: 6g
- Carbs: 16g
- Fiber: 2.5g
- Sugars: 2.5g

69.   Amaranth & Cranberry Bread

Ingredients:

- 1 1/2 cups amaranth flour
- 1/2 cup almond flour
- 1/4 cup dried cranberries
- 2 teaspoons active dry yeast
- 1 teaspoon cinnamon
- 1 tablespoon honey
- 3 large Flaxseed eggs
- 1 1/4 cups warm water
- 1/4 cup olive oil

Instructions:

- ***Combine in the Bread Machine:***
- Place amaranth flour, almond flour, dried cranberries, yeast, and cinnamon into the bread machine.
- ***Prepare Wet Ingredients:***
- In a separate bowl, whisk together honey, Flaxseed eggs, warm water, and olive oil.
- ***Add Wet Ingredients to the Bread Machine:***
- Pour the wet ingredients into the bread machine over the dry ingredients.
- ***Mix in the Bread Machine:***

- Set the bread machine to the gluten-free setting and 2-pound loaf size.
- Press the start button to begin the mixing and kneading process.
- *Pause and Add Mix-Ins:*
- When the machine signals the addition of mix-ins (usually indicated by a beep), add dried cranberries.
- *Complete the Cycle:*
- Allow the machine to run through the entire cycle.
- *Cool and Slice:*
- After the cycle is complete, wait for 10 minutes before carefully removing the bread from the pan.
- Afterwards, transfer the bread to a wire rack and ensure it cools down completely before proceeding with slicing.

Nutritional Information (per slice, calculated for 16 slices):

- Calories: 130
- Protein: 4.5g
- Fat: 6g
- Carbs: 16g
- Fiber: 2.5g
- Sugars: 2.5g

Ingredients:

- 1 1/2 cups quinoa flour
- 1/2 cup almond flour
- 1/4 cup dried blueberries
- 2 teaspoons active dry yeast
- 1 teaspoon cinnamon
- 1 tablespoon honey
- 3 large Flaxseed eggs
- 1 1/4 cups warm water
- 1/4 cup olive oil

Instructions:

- ***Combine in the Bread Machine:***
- Place quinoa flour, almond flour, dried blueberries, yeast, and cinnamon into the bread machine.
- ***Prepare Wet Ingredients:***
- In a separate bowl, whisk together honey, Flaxseed eggs, warm water, and olive oil.
- ***Add Wet Ingredients to the Bread Machine:***
- Pour the wet ingredients into the bread machine over the dry ingredients.
- ***Mix in the Bread Machine:***

- Set the bread machine to the gluten-free setting and 2-pound loaf size.
- Press the start button to begin the mixing and kneading process.
- ***Pause and Add Mix-Ins:***
- When the machine signals the addition of mix-ins (usually indicated by a beep), add dried blueberries.
- ***Complete the Cycle:***
- Allow the machine to run through the entire cycle.
- ***Cool and Slice:***
- After the cycle is complete, wait for 10 minutes before carefully removing the bread from the pan.
- Afterwards, transfer the bread to a wire rack and ensure it cools down completely before proceeding with slicing.

Nutritional Information (per slice, calculated for 16 slices):

- Calories: 130
- Protein: 4.5g
- Fat: 6g
- Carbs: 16g
- Fiber: 2.5g
- Sugars: 2.5g

71. Sesame & Raspberry Bread

Ingredients:

- 1 1/2 cups sesame flour
- 1/2 cup almond flour
- 1/4 cup freeze-dried raspberries, crushed
- 2 teaspoons active dry yeast
- 1 teaspoon cinnamon
- 1 tablespoon honey
- 3 large Flaxseed eggs
- 1 1/4 cups warm water
- 1/4 cup olive oil

Instructions:

- *Combine in the Bread Machine:*
- Place sesame flour, almond flour, crushed freeze-dried raspberries, yeast, and cinnamon into the bread machine.
- *Prepare Wet Ingredients:*
- In a separate bowl, whisk together honey, Flaxseed eggs, warm water, and olive oil.
- *Add Wet Ingredients to the Bread Machine:*
- Pour the wet ingredients into the bread machine over the dry ingredients.
- *Mix in the Bread Machine:*

- Set the bread machine to the gluten-free setting and 2-pound loaf size.
- Press the start button to begin the mixing and kneading process.
- ***Pause and Add Mix-Ins:***
- When the machine signals the addition of mix-ins (usually indicated by a beep), add crushed freeze-dried raspberries.
- ***Complete the Cycle:***
- Allow the machine to run through the entire cycle.
- ***Cool and Slice:***
- After the cycle is complete, wait for 10 minutes before carefully removing the bread from the pan.
- Afterwards, transfer the bread to a wire rack and ensure it cools down completely before proceeding with slicing.

Nutritional Information (per slice, calculated for 16 slices):

- Calories: 130
- Protein: 4.5g
- Fat: 6g
- Carbs: 16g
- Fiber: 2.5g
- Sugars: 2.5g

Ingredients:

- 1 1/2 cups teff flour
- 1/2 cup almond flour
- 1/4 cup dried blackberries
- 2 teaspoons active dry yeast
- 1 teaspoon cinnamon
- 1 tablespoon honey
- 3 large Flaxseed eggs
- 1 1/4 cups warm water
- 1/4 cup olive oil

Instructions:

- *Combine in the Bread Machine:*
- Place teff flour, almond flour, dried blackberries, yeast, and cinnamon into the bread machine.
- *Prepare Wet Ingredients:*
- In a separate bowl, whisk together honey, Flaxseed eggs, warm water, and olive oil.
- *Add Wet Ingredients to the Bread Machine:*
- Pour the wet ingredients into the bread machine over the dry ingredients.
- *Mix in the Bread Machine:*

- Set the bread machine to the gluten-free setting and 2-pound loaf size.
- Press the start button to begin the mixing and kneading process.
- *Pause and Add Mix-Ins:*
- When the machine signals the addition of mix-ins (usually indicated by a beep), add dried blackberries.
- *Complete the Cycle:*
- Allow the machine to run through the entire cycle.
- *Cool and Slice:*
- After the cycle is complete, wait for 10 minutes before carefully removing the bread from the pan.
- Afterwards, transfer the bread to a wire rack and ensure it cools down completely before proceeding with slicing.

Nutritional Information (per slice, calculated for 16 slices):

- Calories: 140
- Protein: 5g
- Fat: 7g
- Carbs: 16g
- Fiber: 3g
- Sugars: 2g

Ingredients:

- 1 1/2 cups buckwheat flour
- 1/2 cup almond flour
- 1/4 cup dried figs, chopped
- 2 teaspoons active dry yeast
- 1 teaspoon salt
- 1 tablespoon honey
- 3 large Flaxseed eggs
- 1 1/4 cups warm water
- 1/4 cup olive oil

Instructions:

- ***Combine in the Bread Machine:***
- Place buckwheat flour, almond flour, chopped dried figs, yeast, and salt into the bread machine.
- ***Prepare Wet Ingredients:***
- In a separate bowl, whisk together honey, Flaxseed eggs, warm water, and olive oil.
- ***Add Wet Ingredients to the Bread Machine:***
- Pour the wet ingredients into the bread machine over the dry ingredients.
- ***Mix in the Bread Machine:***

- Set the bread machine to the gluten-free setting and 2-pound loaf size.
- Press the start button to begin the mixing and kneading process.
- ***Pause and Add Mix-Ins:***
- When the machine signals the addition of mix-ins (usually indicated by a beep), add chopped dried figs.
- ***Complete the Cycle:***
- Allow the machine to run through the entire cycle.
- ***Cool and Slice:***
- After the cycle is complete, wait for 10 minutes before carefully removing the bread from the pan.
- Afterwards, transfer the bread to a wire rack and ensure it cools down completely before proceeding with slicing.

Nutritional Information (per slice, calculated for 16 slices):

- Calories: 140
- Protein: 5g
- Fat: 7g
- Carbs: 16g
- Fiber: 3g
- Sugars: 2g

74. Quinoa & Apricot Bread

Ingredients:

- 1 1/2 cups quinoa flour
- 1/2 cup almond flour
- 1/4 cup chopped dried apricots
- 2 teaspoons active dry yeast
- 1 teaspoon cinnamon
- 1 tablespoon honey
- 3 large Flaxseed eggs
- 1 1/4 cups warm water
- 1/4 cup olive oil

Instructions:

- *Combine in the Bread Machine:*
- Place quinoa flour, almond flour, chopped dried apricots, yeast, and cinnamon into the bread machine.
- *Prepare Wet Ingredients:*
- In a separate bowl, whisk together honey, Flaxseed eggs, warm water, and olive oil.
- *Add Wet Ingredients to the Bread Machine:*
- Pour the wet ingredients into the bread machine over the dry ingredients.
- *Mix in the Bread Machine:*

- Set the bread machine to the gluten-free setting and 2-pound loaf size.
- Press the start button to begin the mixing and kneading process.
- ***Pause and Add Mix-Ins:***
- When the machine signals the addition of mix-ins (usually indicated by a beep), add chopped dried apricots.
- ***Complete the Cycle:***
- Allow the machine to run through the entire cycle.
- ***Cool and Slice:***
- After the cycle is complete, wait for 10 minutes before carefully removing the bread from the pan.
- Afterwards, transfer the bread to a wire rack and ensure it cools down completely before proceeding with slicing.

Nutritional Information (per slice, calculated for 16 slices):

- Calories: 140
- Protein: 5g
- Fat: 7g
- Carbs: 16g
- Fiber: 3g
- Sugars: 2g

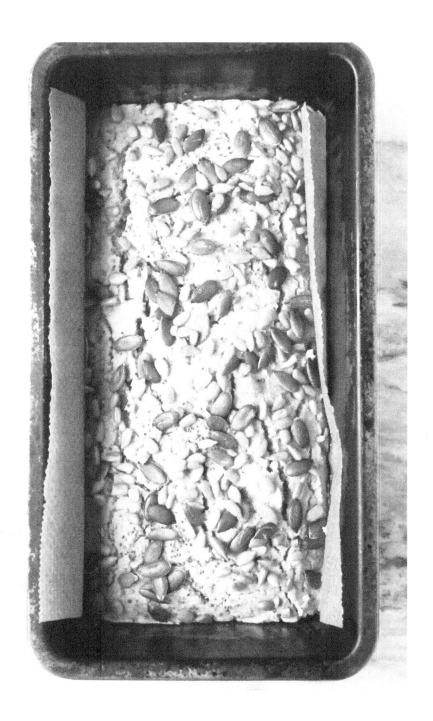

Gluten-Free Bread Machine Tips and Troubleshooting

Tips for Making Gluten-Free Bread in a Bread Machine:

Use a Gluten-Free Bread Machine Setting: Many bread machines have a specific gluten-free setting. This setting usually has a longer kneading time and extra rising cycles, which help develop the structure and texture of gluten-free bread. If your bread machine doesn't have a gluten-free setting, choose a setting with a longer mixing and rising time.

Follow a Reliable Gluten-Free Recipe: It's essential to use a reliable gluten-free bread recipe specifically made for a bread machine. Gluten-free bread needs different ingredients and ratios compared to traditional wheat-based bread. Look for recipes that have been tested and reviewed by others to improve your chances of success.

Choose the Right Gluten-Free Flour Blend: Gluten-free bread flour blends are easily available in stores, or you can make your own blend. Look for a blend that includes a mixture of flours such as rice flour, tapioca flour, potato starch, and xanthan gum. Experiment with different blends to find the one that gives the best texture and flavor for your taste.

Measure Ingredients Accurately: Gluten-free baking is more sensitive to ingredient ratios, so it's crucial to measure ingredients correctly. Use measuring cups and spoons specifically made for dry or wet ingredients, and level off the excess to ensure consistency in your recipe.

Add Xanthan Gum or Guar Gum*:* Xanthan gum or guar gum is often added to gluten-free bread recipes to help improve the texture and structure. These ingredients act as a binder and mimic the flexibility of gluten. Follow the recipe steps for the recommended amount of xanthan gum or guar gum to add to your dough.

Adjust Liquid and Flour Ratios: Gluten-free bread dough tends to be stickier and more fluid than standard bread dough. Depending on the individual recipe and flour blend you're using, you may need to adjust the liquid and flour ratios slightly. If the dough looks too dry, add a tablespoon of water at a time until it reaches the desired consistency. If the dough is too wet and sticky, add a tablespoon of flour at a time until it becomes easier to handle.

Allow for Extra Rising Time: Gluten-free bread often needs additional rising time compared to traditional bread. This extra time helps the dough to develop structure and improve the texture. If your bread machine allows it, you can manually add an extra rise step or two to the baking process.

Troubleshooting Gluten-Free Bread Machine Issues:

Dense or Heavy Bread: If your gluten-free bread turns out dense or heavy, it could be due to several reasons. First, make sure you're using the correct flour blend with the proper ratios. Additionally, check that you're using enough liquid in the recipe and that the dough has sufficient rising time. Overmixing the dough or using too much flour can also result in a thick texture.

Bread falls or Sinks in the Middle: If your gluten-free bread falls or sinks in the middle, it could be due to insufficient structure development. Ensure you're using the recommended amount of xanthan gum or guar gum in the recipe. Over-proofing the dough or using too much yeast can also cause collapsing, so be careful of rising times and yeast quantities.

Crumbly or Dry Texture: A crumbly or dry texture in your gluten-free bread can be a result of using too much flour or not enough fluids. Check your measurements and adjust properly. Adding a small amount of fat, such as olive oil or melted butter, can also help improve the moisture content and structure of the bread.

sticky or Doughy Center: If your gluten-free bread has a sticky or doughy center, it may be underbaked. Ensure that you're baking the bread for the recommended time and that your oven temperature is correct. You can also check the core temperature of the bread using an instant-read thermometer. The internal temperature should hit around 200°F (93°C) to ensure its fully baked.

Bread Sticks to the Pan: Gluten-free bread dough can be stickier than traditional dough, making it more prone to sticking to the bread machine pan. To avoid this, make sure the bread machine pan is well-greased before adding the dough. You can use non-stick food spray or grease it with oil or butter. Additionally, using a pan liner or parchment paper can also help avoid sticking.

Uneven Rising or Shaping: If your gluten-free bread machine rolls or buns have uneven rising or shaping, make sure you're dividing the dough into equal parts. Use a kitchen scale to weigh each amount for consistency. Additionally, ensure that the rolls or buns are placed with enough room between them on the baking sheet to allow for proper rising.

Adjusting Recipes for Altitude or Climate: If you live in a high-altitude area or a humid climate, you may need to make changes to your gluten-free bread machine recipes. At high altitudes, you may need to lower the amount of yeast slightly and increase the baking temperature or time. In humid climates, you may need to lower the liquid slightly and increase the baking time to achieve the desired texture.

Remember that gluten-free baking can be a bit more challenging and may require some experimentation to find the perfect mix of ingredients and techniques that work for you. Don't get discouraged if your first few attempts don't turn out as planned. With practice and changes, you'll soon be able to bake delicious gluten-free bread in your bread machine.

Storing and Freezing Gluten-Free Bread

Storing Gluten-Free Bread:

Airtight Containers: When it comes to keeping gluten-free bread, I've found that using airtight containers works best. I prefer using a bread box or a plastic container with a tight-sealing lid. This helps to keep the moisture and freshness of the bread, preventing it from becoming dry or stale.

Avoid the Refrigerator: Unlike traditional wheat bread, I suggest avoiding storing gluten-free bread in the refrigerator. The cold weather can cause the bread to become dry and lose its soft texture more quickly. Instead, find a cool, dry spot in your kitchen or closet to store the bread at room temperature.

Slicing and Freezing Extra Loaves: If I have multiple loaves of gluten-free bread or won't be able to eat them all within a few days, I slice the extra loaves before storing them. Sliced bread freezes and thaws more easily, allowing me to take out only the number of slices I need without having to thaw the entire loaf.

Freezer-Safe Bags: For freezing sliced gluten-free bread, I individually wrap each slice in plastic wrap or parchment paper before putting them in a freezer-safe bag. This way, I can quickly grab one or two slices at a time without having to defrost the entire package. It also helps to avoid freezer burn and maintain the bread's freshness.

mark and Date: To keep track of the freezing time and ensure that I use the oldest bread first, I mark each bag or container with the date of freezing. This helps me avoid having the bread sit in the freezer for too long, ensuring that I enjoy it at its best quality.

Thawing and Refreshing Gluten-Free Bread:

Room Temperature Thawing: When I want to enjoy frozen gluten-free bread, I take out the appropriate number of slices or the whole loaf from the freezer and let them thaw at room temperature. This usually takes a couple of hours, based on the thickness of the slices. I avoid defrosting the bread in the microwave or using hot water, as it can lead to uneven melting and make the bread soggy.

Toasting for Freshness: If the thawed gluten-free bread feels slightly dry or stale, I find that toasting it helps revive its texture and taste. I use a toaster or a toaster oven and adjust the settings to my desired level of toasting. The gentle heat and small crisping of the bread make it taste almost as good as freshly baked.

Enjoying Freshly Thawed Bread: Once the gluten-free bread has thawed and been toasted, I like to enjoy it within a day or two for the best taste and texture. If there are leftover slices, I put them in an airtight container at room temperature for a day or two. However, I find that gluten-free bread is best enjoyed fresh or soon after thawing.

Experiment with Storage Methods: Everyone's kitchen environment and tastes may differ, so I encourage you to experiment with different storage methods to find what works best for you. Try using different types of containers or bags to see which one help keep the freshness of your gluten-free bread the longest.

Quality Ingredients and Recipes: Using high-quality gluten-free flour blends and reliable recipes can make a major difference in the texture and shelf life of your bread. Experiment with different flour blends and recipes until you find the ones that give the best results for your taste and dietary needs.

Consider Freshly Baked Alternatives: While freezing gluten-free bread can be handy, there's nothing quite like the taste and texture of freshly baked bread. If time permits, I often prefer baking smaller amounts more frequently to enjoy the bread at its peak freshness.

Communication with Bakery: If baking gluten-free bread at home isn't an option, I recommend communicating with local bakeries or specialty shops that offer gluten-free choices. Inquire about their storage recommendations and ask if they have any specific instructions for keeping the freshness of their gluten-free bread.

Remember, each person's experience with keeping and freezing gluten-free bread may vary. These tips and personal views can serve as a starting point, but feel free to adapt them to your own preferences and circumstances. With some experimentation and attention to storage methods, you can enjoy delicious gluten-free bread for longer times without compromising its quality.

Conclusion

Dear Reader,

I want to take a moment to express my heartfelt gratitude for choosing to start on this gluten-free bread machine journey with me through the pages of "Gluten-Free Bread Machine Cookbook." It fills my heart with joy to know that you've joined me on this delicious adventure, discovering the magical world of gluten-free baking.

Writing this cookbook has been a labor of love, fueled by my own personal experiences, successes, and even a few baking mishaps along the way. I wanted to create a book that not only provides you with mouthwatering recipes but also serves as a trusted friend, guiding you through the exciting process of baking gluten-free bread with a bread machine.

As you turn the pages, I hope you feel the emotion and dedication that went into each recipe. I've poured my heart into choosing the finest ingredients, experimenting with different flour blends, and perfecting the techniques to ensure that every loaf you bake is a masterpiece. It's been a wonderful journey of trial and error, learning from each batch, and refining the recipes to bring you the best possible results.

But this cookbook isn't just about food. It's about empowering you to become a successful gluten-free baker. Throughout the book, I've shared personal thoughts, tips, and tricks that I've picked up along the way. I want you to feel like we're standing side by side in the kitchen, learning the art of gluten-free bread baking together.

I encourage you to make these meals your own. Feel free to experiment with different flavors, add your favorite mix-ins, and adapt them to fit your dietary needs and cravings. Baking should be a joyous and creative experience, and I hope that this cookbook sparks your mind and inspires you to create your own gluten-free bread masterpieces.

Lastly, I want to show my deepest gratitude to you, the reader. Your help and enthusiasm mean the world to me. It is your excitement that fuels my love for sharing the wonders of gluten-free bread baking. Thank you for being a part of this amazing journey, and I can't wait to hear about your baking adventures and the joy that comes with each successful loaf.

Happy baking!

With heartfelt thanks,

Megan!

Bonus Pages Up Next

My Recipe Planner

NAME OF RECIPE

INGREDIENTS

DIFFICULTY

SERVES _____

METHOD

PREP TIME _____

REVIEW ☆ ☆ ☆ ☆ ☆

◯ **CLASSIC**

◯ **SOURDOUGH**

◯ **DAIRY FREE**

◯ **SPECIALTY**

◯ **VEGAN**

NOTES:

◯ **ARTISAN**

◯ **QUICK AND EASY**

◯ **GLUTEN - FREE**

Mix, Bake, Conquer

My Recipe Planner

NAME OF RECIPE

INGREDIENTS

DIFFICULTY

SERVES _____

METHOD

PREP TIME _____

REVIEW ☆ ☆ ☆ ☆ ☆

◯ CLASSIC

◯ SOURDOUGH

◯ DAIRY FREE

◯ SPECIALTY

◯ VEGAN

NOTES:

◯ ARTISAN

◯ QUICK AND EASY

◯ GLUTEN - FREE

M i x ,   B a k e ,   C o n q u e r

My Recipe Planner

NAME OF RECIPE

INGREDIENTS

DIFFICULTY

SERVES _____

METHOD

PREP TIME _____

REVIEW ☆ ☆ ☆ ☆ ☆

○ CLASSIC

○ SOURDOUGH

○ DAIRY FREE

○ SPECIALTY

○ VEGAN

NOTES:

○ ARTISAN

○ QUICK AND EASY

○ GLUTEN - FREE

Mix, Bake, Conquer

My Recipe Planner

NAME OF RECIPE

INGREDIENTS

DIFFICULTY

SERVES _____

METHOD

PREP TIME _____

REVIEW ☆ ☆ ☆ ☆ ☆

○ CLASSIC

○ SOURDOUGH

○ DAIRY FREE

○ SPECIALTY

○ VEGAN

NOTES:

○ ARTISAN

○ QUICK AND EASY

○ GLUTEN - FREE

Mix, Bake, Conquer

My Recipe Planner

NAME OF RECIPE

INGREDIENTS

DIFFICULTY

SERVES _____

METHOD

PREP TIME _____

REVIEW ☆ ☆ ☆ ☆ ☆

○ **CLASSIC**

○ **SOURDOUGH**

○ **DAIRY FREE**

○ **SPECIALTY**

○ **VEGAN**

NOTES:

○ **ARTISAN**

○ **QUICK AND EASY**

○ **GLUTEN – FREE**

M i x ,   B a k e ,   C o n q u e r

My Recipe Planner

NAME OF RECIPE

INGREDIENTS

DIFFICULTY

SERVES _____

METHOD

PREP TIME _____

REVIEW ☆ ☆ ☆ ☆ ☆

○ CLASSIC

○ SOURDOUGH

○ DAIRY FREE

○ SPECIALTY

○ VEGAN

NOTES:

○ ARTISAN

○ QUICK AND EASY

○ GLUTEN - FREE

Mix, Bake, Conquer

My Recipe Planner

NAME OF RECIPE

INGREDIENTS

_____   _____
_____   _____
_____   _____

DIFFICULTY

○ ○ ○ ○ ○

_____   _____
_____   _____
_____   _____

METHOD

SERVES _____

_____
_____

PREP TIME _____

_____
_____

REVIEW ☆ ☆ ☆ ☆ ☆

_____
_____
_____

○ CLASSIC

_____

○ SOURDOUGH

_____

○ DAIRY FREE

_____

○ SPECIALTY

_____

○ VEGAN

NOTES:

○ ARTISAN

_____

○ QUICK AND EASY

_____

○ GLUTEN - FREE

_____
_____
_____

Mix, Bake, Conquer

My Recipe Planner

NAME OF RECIPE

INGREDIENTS

DIFFICULTY

SERVES _____

METHOD

PREP TIME _____

REVIEW ☆ ☆ ☆ ☆ ☆

◯ **CLASSIC**

◯ **SOURDOUGH**

◯ **DAIRY FREE**

◯ **SPECIALTY**

◯ **VEGAN**

NOTES:

◯ **ARTISAN**

◯ **QUICK AND EASY**

◯ **GLUTEN - FREE**

M i x ,   B a k e ,   C o n q u e r

My Recipe Planner

NAME OF RECIPE

INGREDIENTS

DIFFICULTY

SERVES _____

METHOD

PREP TIME _____

REVIEW ☆ ☆ ☆ ☆ ☆

○ CLASSIC

○ SOURDOUGH

○ DAIRY FREE

○ SPECIALTY

○ VEGAN

NOTES:

○ ARTISAN

○ QUICK AND EASY

○ GLUTEN - FREE

Mix, Bake, Conquer

My Recipe Planner

NAME OF RECIPE

INGREDIENTS

DIFFICULTY

SERVES _____

METHOD

PREP TIME _____

REVIEW ☆ ☆ ☆ ☆ ☆

○ **CLASSIC**

○ **SOURDOUGH**

○ **DAIRY FREE**

○ **SPECIALTY**

○ **VEGAN**

NOTES:

○ **ARTISAN**

○ **QUICK AND EASY**

○ **GLUTEN - FREE**

M i x ,   B a k e ,   C o n q u e r

My Recipe Planner

NAME OF RECIPE

INGREDIENTS

DIFFICULTY

⬤ ⬤ ⬤ ⬤ ⬤

SERVES _____

METHOD

PREP TIME _____

REVIEW ☆ ☆ ☆ ☆ ☆

◯ CLASSIC

◯ SOURDOUGH

◯ DAIRY FREE

◯ SPECIALTY

◯ VEGAN

NOTES:

◯ ARTISAN

◯ QUICK AND EASY

◯ GLUTEN - FREE

Mix, Bake, Conquer

My Recipe Planner

NAME OF RECIPE

INGREDIENTS

DIFFICULTY

○ ○ ○ ○ ○

SERVES _____

METHOD

PREP TIME _____

REVIEW ☆ ☆ ☆ ☆ ☆

○ CLASSIC

○ SOURDOUGH

○ DAIRY FREE

○ SPECIALTY

○ VEGAN

NOTES:

○ ARTISAN

○ QUICK AND EASY

○ GLUTEN – FREE

Mix, Bake, Conquer

My Recipe Planner

NAME OF RECIPE

INGREDIENTS

DIFFICULTY

SERVES _____

METHOD

PREP TIME _____

REVIEW ☆ ☆ ☆ ☆ ☆

○ CLASSIC

○ SOURDOUGH

○ DAIRY FREE

○ SPECIALTY

○ VEGAN

NOTES:

○ ARTISAN

○ QUICK AND EASY

○ GLUTEN - FREE

Mix, Bake, Conquer

My Recipe Planner

NAME OF RECIPE

INGREDIENTS

DIFFICULTY

SERVES _____

METHOD

PREP TIME _____

REVIEW ☆ ☆ ☆ ☆ ☆

○ CLASSIC

○ SOURDOUGH

○ DAIRY FREE

○ SPECIALTY

○ VEGAN

NOTES:

○ ARTISAN

○ QUICK AND EASY

○ GLUTEN - FREE

Mix, Bake, Conquer

My Recipe Planner

NAME OF RECIPE

INGREDIENTS

DIFFICULTY

● ● ● ● ●

SERVES _____

METHOD

PREP TIME _____

REVIEW ☆ ☆ ☆ ☆ ☆

○ CLASSIC

○ SOURDOUGH

○ DAIRY FREE

○ SPECIALTY

○ VEGAN

NOTES:

○ ARTISAN

○ QUICK AND EASY

○ GLUTEN - FREE

Mix, Bake, Conquer

My Recipe Planner

NAME OF RECIPE

INGREDIENTS

DIFFICULTY

SERVES _____

METHOD

PREP TIME _____

REVIEW ☆ ☆ ☆ ☆ ☆

○ CLASSIC

○ SOURDOUGH

○ DAIRY FREE

○ SPECIALTY

○ VEGAN

NOTES:

○ ARTISAN

○ QUICK AND EASY

○ GLUTEN – FREE

Mix, Bake, Conquer

My Recipe Planner

NAME OF RECIPE

INGREDIENTS

DIFFICULTY

SERVES _____

METHOD

PREP TIME _____

REVIEW ☆ ☆ ☆ ☆ ☆

○ CLASSIC

○ SOURDOUGH

○ DAIRY FREE

○ SPECIALTY

○ VEGAN

NOTES:

○ ARTISAN

○ QUICK AND EASY

○ GLUTEN - FREE

M i x ,   B a k e ,   C o n q u e r

My Recipe Planner

NAME OF RECIPE

INGREDIENTS

DIFFICULTY

SERVES _____

METHOD

PREP TIME _____

REVIEW ☆ ☆ ☆ ☆ ☆

◯ **CLASSIC**

◯ **SOURDOUGH**

◯ **DAIRY FREE**

◯ **SPECIALTY**

◯ **VEGAN**

NOTES:

◯ **ARTISAN**

◯ **QUICK AND EASY**

◯ **GLUTEN – FREE**

M i x ,   B a k e ,   C o n q u e r

My Recipe Planner

NAME OF RECIPE

INGREDIENTS

DIFFICULTY

○ ○ ○ ○ ○

SERVES _____

METHOD

PREP TIME _____

REVIEW ☆ ☆ ☆ ☆ ☆

○ CLASSIC

○ SOURDOUGH

○ DAIRY FREE

○ SPECIALTY

○ VEGAN

NOTES:

○ ARTISAN

○ QUICK AND EASY

○ GLUTEN - FREE

Mix, Bake, Conquer

My Recipe Planner

NAME OF RECIPE

INGREDIENTS

DIFFICULTY

SERVES _____

METHOD

PREP TIME _____

REVIEW ☆ ☆ ☆ ☆ ☆

○ CLASSIC
○ SOURDOUGH
○ DAIRY FREE
○ SPECIALTY
○ VEGAN
○ ARTISAN
○ QUICK AND EASY
○ GLUTEN - FREE

NOTES:

Mix, Bake, Conquer

My Recipe Planner

NAME OF RECIPE

INGREDIENTS

DIFFICULTY

SERVES _____

METHOD

PREP TIME _____

REVIEW ☆ ☆ ☆ ☆ ☆

◯ CLASSIC

◯ SOURDOUGH

◯ DAIRY FREE

◯ SPECIALTY

◯ VEGAN

NOTES:

◯ ARTISAN

◯ QUICK AND EASY

◯ GLUTEN - FREE

Mix, Bake, Conquer

My Recipe Planner

NAME OF RECIPE

INGREDIENTS

_____   _____
_____   _____
_____   _____

DIFFICULTY

⬤ ⬤ ⬤ ⬤ ⬤

METHOD

SERVES _____

PREP TIME _____

REVIEW ☆ ☆ ☆ ☆ ☆

◯ CLASSIC

◯ SOURDOUGH

◯ DAIRY FREE

◯ SPECIALTY

◯ VEGAN

NOTES:

◯ ARTISAN

◯ QUICK AND EASY

◯ GLUTEN – FREE

Mix, Bake, Conquer

My Recipe Planner

NAME OF RECIPE

INGREDIENTS

_____ _____
_____ _____
_____ _____
_____ _____

DIFFICULTY

● ● ● ● ●

SERVES _____

METHOD

_____
_____

PREP TIME _____

_____
_____

REVIEW ☆ ☆ ☆ ☆ ☆

_____
_____

○ CLASSIC

_____

○ SOURDOUGH

_____

○ DAIRY FREE

_____

○ SPECIALTY

_____

○ VEGAN

NOTES:

○ ARTISAN

_____

○ QUICK AND EASY

_____

○ GLUTEN – FREE

_____

Mix, Bake, Conquer

My Recipe Planner

NAME OF RECIPE

INGREDIENTS

DIFFICULTY

SERVES _____

METHOD

PREP TIME _____

REVIEW ☆ ☆ ☆ ☆ ☆

○ CLASSIC

○ SOURDOUGH

○ DAIRY FREE

○ SPECIALTY

○ VEGAN

NOTES:

○ ARTISAN

○ QUICK AND EASY

○ GLUTEN - FREE

M i x ,   B a k e ,   C o n q u e r